WALKING
TO
WISDOM

David Voss

WALKING TO WISDOM

David Voss

E-BookTime, LLC
Montgomery, Alabama

WALKING TO WISDOM

Copyright © 2005 by David Voss

All rights reserved. No part of this book may be reproduced or transmitted in any form or by any means, electronic or mechanical, including photocopying, recording, or by any information storage and retrieval system, without permission in writing from the copyright owner.

Library of Congress Control Number: 2005934332

ISBN: 1-59824-081-1

First Edition
Published September 2005
E-BookTime, LLC
6598 Pumpkin Road
Montgomery, AL 36108
www.e-booktime.com

For Lynn

ACKNOWLEDGMENTS

Many people have contributed to my getting my act together enough to produce a book. For reasons best known to myself, I have been delaying such a project for many years in spite of the encouragement of family and friends. I must thank, or blame, David Wiseman for my finally getting something into print. I am not quite sure why his word broke the logjam – perhaps the timing of his own decision to "do something" or perhaps the fact that I had just turned seventy. In any event it worked.

I am also grateful to my wife Lynn, who has listened to me talk or read my ramblings for over forty years. She has gifted me with encouragement, candid commentary and persistent reminders of my equally persistent flaws in punctuation. Since she offered to edit this collection, I can confidently thank her for its final grammatical form. Whatever flaws may have crept into the printed version were due more to my insistence than her diligence.

I cannot name everyone else who gave me a word of encouragement. A few whose words have meant a lot to me are Jane, Ellen, Kate, Geneva, Charlyn, Betty, Harding, Suzanne, Charles, Ruth, Ann, Allen, Chuck, Jeannette, Tom, Gary, Bob, Jeannene, Owen, and Dan. If your name is not here, thank you and forgive me.

THE LONG WALK TO WISDOM

My father was not given to reminiscence. Only the barest outlines of his childhood reached my ears, even less of his young manhood. I often wondered why he kept his story so closely guarded. I scrambled quickly for whatever small pearls he might drop and strung them together as best I could.

One story I heard more than once, which makes it especially memorable. It is not exactly a story, for it never went anywhere. In fact, that seemed to be the point. From time to time, when we visited with his sisters, my father would share memories with them about walking many miles to a small country school with the unlikely name of "Wisdom." He liked to talk about how long and how cold were the miles. In fact they seemed to get longer and colder with each telling, sometimes augmented with extra hardships by one particular sister, an amiably oversized woman with the even more unlikely name of Flossie Myrtle. He and Aunt Flossie talked and laughed about the long walk through the snow to Wisdom. (Even as a child I was skeptical about the depth of the snow, since my father's home in South Georgia was not noted for its white Christmases.)

But I never doubted that there was indeed a school called Wisdom. Nor did I doubt that it was there that my father became the wise person that I know him to be. It even struck me as amazingly symbolic, if somewhat whimsical, that Wisdom was the name of the school. My father's long walk to Wisdom became for me a kind of rough metaphor for "learning acquired the hard way." Try as I may I cannot recall anything of what either he or Flossie Myrtle actually learned when they got to Wisdom. The walk seemed more memorable to them than the school itself. Perhaps again there was an unintended lesson. Education consists more in what is experienced along the way than in what is imposed inside the walls. I have sometimes thought that experience plus insight equals epiphany. Perhaps epiphany tested by further experience eventually equals wisdom.

    I have begun to gather recollections and reflections that constitute some of what I have discovered during my long walk toward Wisdom. At this point I cannot say that I know what that mythical place actually looks like any more than I ever saw a picture of my father's childhood school. What I have collected is a mix of personal memoirs, sermons and essays written during my years as a pastoral counselor. I believe that the sermons and essays are informed by personal experience as well as by what I have learned from many men and women, past and present, who also took that walk. If, after grazing from the pages that follow, you are curious about my current perspective on just how long that walk may be, you are invited to read my final little essay. In the meantime, enjoy the walk.

BUMPS IN THE ROAD

As for life, it is a battle and a sojourning in a strange land...the art of living is more like wrestling than dancing.
-Marcus Aurelius

He who would valiant be 'gainst all disaster,
Let him in constancy follow the Master.
There's no discouragement shall make him once relent
His first avowed intent to be a pilgrim.
-John Bunyan

IN HARM'S WAY

I saw that under the sun the race is not always to the swift, nor the battle to the strong, nor bread to the wise, nor riches to the intelligent, nor favor to the skillful; but time and chance happen to them all.
Ecclesiastes 9:11

The Son of Man must undergo great suffering . . . if any want to become my followers, let them deny themselves and take up their cross daily and follow me . . .
Luke 9:21-22

Not long ago the gospel lesson on a Sunday morning included Jesus' words in Nazareth, where he spoke of preaching "release to the captives." A very thoughtful man approached me after church and asked, "Doesn't that mean letting some criminals out that might do harm?" A few weeks ago when I preached about welcoming the stranger, a thoughtful woman reminded me, "But sometimes if you befriend a stranger that stranger may turn on you and hurt you." To both of these thoughtful objections I can only say, "Yes, indeed. There is definitely a risk in doing what Jesus says and does. Yes, mixing with sinners may mean getting your pocket picked."

What concerned my thoughtful questioners, I think, was the notion of deliberately choosing to put ourselves "in harm's way." Does being a Christian mean making ourselves more vulnerable than we already are? I want you to think with me about what it means to be vulnerable. The word means "capable of being wounded." At least since the time of that preacher known as Ecclesiastes, men and women have thought and spoken and written about just how vulnerable we are.

I

Just being alive makes us vulnerable. To aging, to illness, to accident, to the uncertain and seemingly random intrusions that the insurance companies like to call "acts of God." The ancient preacher put it in these poignant words: *The race is not always to the swift, nor the battle to the strong, nor bread to the wise, nor riches to the intelligent, nor favor to the skillful; but time and chance happen to them all.* More recently an American writer named Wendell Berry put it this way, "We all have to live through enough to kill us."

Being alive makes us vulnerable, vulnerable to time and chance. Some are more vulnerable than others. Children are more vulnerable, so are those with disabilities, and those who have been weakened with the passing of years. Part of the measure of our humanity is seen in how we deal with the vulnerability of others. Harry Emerson Fosdick said, "the basic test of a society is what happens to the underdog."

Being human makes us vulnerable in many other ways. In September 2001 we discovered that we Americans are more vulnerable than we used to think. But this vulnerability, that is new and frightening to us, is an old familiar story to the rest of humanity. Just think of all the ways being human makes us vulnerable.

We need security, so we are vulnerable to those who can hurt us or those whom we love. We need friendship, so we are vulnerable to rejection, betrayal, indifference. We need companionship, so we are vulnerable to the loss of those we love. I think it was Ernest Hemingway who said that every marriage ends unhappily, for someone is always left alone by his or her beloved. We need a sense of worth, so we are vulnerable to failure and to the judgment of others who may see us as failures. We need to know that our life has meaning and purpose, so we are vulnerable to the fear that meaning will elude us.

Finally *being Christian makes us vulnerable.* We put ourselves in harm's way by the choices we make. If you choose to forgive someone who has hurt you, you are vulnerable to being hurt again and looking like a fool. If I choose to give a gift to someone, whether money or time or energy, I am vulnerable. I may be exploited, used, or, at the least, unappreciated. If we choose to pay attention to the pain of our neighbor, then we are vulnerable to feeling some of that pain. Jesus isn't kidding when he says that following him is like bearing a cross. Loving people who aren't always loveable can definitely put us in harm's way.

II

So, vulnerability is a fact of human life. How we deal with it is a choice we make every day, a choice that determines the kind of persons we are going to become, in fact are already becoming. Think about some of the ways we deal with our hurts and with our vulnerability to hurt. I can think of three. Call them indifference, revenge, and addiction.

We can protect ourselves by putting on the armor of indifference. As Simon and Garfunkel put it in one of their songs, "I am a rock. I am an island. A rock feels no pain and an island never cries." One way to deal with the hurts of being human is to deny them as best we can. Or to keep people from getting close enough to mean much to us. Certainly plenty of people practice this; we all use denial or distance some of the time for dealing with more pain than we think we can handle. The price we pay for the armor of indifference is the price of isolation and the numbness of an unrealized life.

We can compensate for our hurts with what we call the sweetness of revenge. We can try to make ourselves feel better by getting back at those who hurt us. Of course we can't get back at life for hurting us, but we spend a lot of time trying at least to get back at people. We spend our energy feeding our resentment and looking for ways to get even.

Certainly that is the root of most of the violence between nations as well as the never-ending feuds that poison families – sometimes long after the members no longer live under the same roof. We are always wanting to "make someone pay" for what they have done to us, either legally or personally. Let's face it; what we like to call our desire for justice is often simply a longing for revenge, for satisfaction, for something that we think will take away the pain we have suffered.

Of course the sad outcome of such sagas of resentment is that revenge is never enough to take away our pain. Our hurt is never satisfied by our revenge, for our hurt always seems greater than any we can inflict in return. Just ask someone who has lost a loved one to a violent crime or to war. They know that retaliation or justice or revenge does not bring back the loved one. It is not true that "revenge is sweet." Revenge is not sweet. Revenge is bitter. And revenge leaves a legacy of bitterness even in those who think they have "gotten even."

One more way. *We can try to medicate our hurts with the false comfort of addiction.* If we cannot get away from the world or get back at the world, we can at least try to console ourselves with short-term comforts. You might call addiction a quick way to feel better that finally makes you feel worse.

We think of addiction in terms of alcohol or drugs or food. But it is really much broader than that. Accumulating money can be an addiction. So can sports, or shopping, or sex. What these pastimes have in common is the *way we explain them to ourselves*. We tell ourselves that we *need* them. In fact we *deserve* them because of all the hard things we have had to put up with. How many affairs are born of that feeling of being misunderstood; how many binges – of drinking or shopping – do we justify because we've "had a bad day"? This is what someone has called "negative entitlement." It goes like this: "the world has treated me badly, so I'm entitled to something to make myself feel better."

The price of addiction? Our remedies are never enough, and never long enough. We remain unhappy, not to mention carrying an extra layer of guilt for our efforts at a quick fix. Our ways of dealing with pain all carry a heavy price – whether we resort to the armor of indifference, the bitter sweetness of revenge, or the false comfort of addiction.

III

So, is there a better way to deal with our vulnerability as human beings and as Christians? I think that there is. I'm afraid it is not going to be easy. We can ask, as some of our fellow Christians today might ask, "what would Jesus do?" Or better, what *did* Jesus do? What do we see when we look at the one who was, we say, most fully human?

First, we see that Jesus accepted the pain of life as a part of life. You might put his attitude this way: "I accept what it means to be human and what it costs to be loving." Accepting the pain of life means understanding that we have no right to think that life should be less painful for us than it is for any of God's other children. It means letting go of the idea that we cannot stand it unless we get above it, or get even, or get numb. Time and chance do happen to us all, and some other hard things too, if we choose to be human enough to reach out to others in love.

Second, he shared it. Jesus did not keep his sadness to himself like a stoic or a movie cowboy. We are told that he wept with those who wept; he spoke to his followers of his hopes for them and of his disappointments; he gave voice to his anger instead of acting it out in violence or revenge. Accepting our share of the suffering of the world does not mean resigning ourselves to a life of stoic loneliness. If we are willing to be vulnerable to others with our pain, we can ask them to share it with us.

Finally, Jesus allowed the hurts of life, including the ones he willingly took on himself, to make him a larger person – more compassionate, more forgiving, more able to embrace the suffering of his fellow humans.

We all stand in harm's way every day of our lives. Vulnerability is a fact of life for each of us. Our choice is not *whether* we will deal with vulnerability but *how*. And the choices that we make every day will slowly shape that internal foundation that we call character. They may make us bitter or cynical, self-indulgent or numb. Or they can help us become more humane, more compassionate, more generous, more Christian.

Time and chance happen to us all. Suffering and losses and crosses too. Our challenge is to respond to them as men and women of faith who have chosen to follow the way that points us toward a fuller life.

SELF-INFLICTED WOUNDS

During a visit to our home in Virginia some years ago, my mother, a widow in her early seventies, suffered a stroke that left her partially paralyzed and totally speechless for the last eight years of her life.

In the first days after the stroke her survival was very much in doubt – so much so that Lynn and I spent time planning a funeral service before the anticipated trip to Georgia for burial. There were many difficult hours in ICU, watching the monitors flicker behind her bed, wondering whether and when the moving line on the screen would go flat. There were agonizing doubts as to whether it might, in fact, be better if it did.

To add a layer of anger and remorse to the occasion, there was the fact that my mother's stroke had occurred in the aftermath of a sharp argument between us – an argument that she ended with the words, "I'm not going to talk about it anymore." Those were, in fact, the last intelligible words my mother spoke – to me or to anyone else – in the last eight years of her life. Her final words became a grimly self-fulfilling prophecy. In the days following her stroke I had no way of knowing that there would be times when I could speak to her and she could return some signs of understanding and even affection. In those first days there was only a huge unfinished question mark hanging over our relationship.

It was in this climate that I decided to go ahead with a scheduled appointment that I had long awaited and dreaded. Three days after Mother's stroke I was scheduled to meet with a three person committee which would approve me, or disapprove me, for membership in the American Association of Pastoral Counselors. It was an important step for me professionally, and a somewhat scary one. Such meetings were known to be challenging and sometimes devastating. I had sent forward all the required paperwork and the taped interviews which we would discuss. In a shaky sort of way I was ready.

When I decided to keep my scheduled appointment in spite of my family crisis, I also decided to tell no one on the committee of my mother's condition or my own state of mind. In some warped way I felt that that would not be "right." I would, I resolved, try to pull it off in the best stoic tradition.

The details of the committee meeting are too painful to recount. Let it suffice to say that my stoicism was overwhelmed by my depression, that I had about as much mental and verbal agility as my paralyzed and aphasic Mother. I was turned down, of course, by three puzzled pastoral counselors who could not figure out what was wrong with me. One man spoke to me in private as he wished me better luck next time. "Was something bothering you today?" When I called Lynn to tell her of my misadventure, I was able finally to release some of the tears of my accumulated pain.

A few weeks later, when I had had time to gather some of the pieces of my self-esteem, I met with an old mentor to talk about how to prepare for the "next time." I told him my sad story, including the story of my mother and of my deliberate choice of silence. He smiled and shook his head. "You don't trust people much, do you?"

My silence, I have come to understand, did have a lot to do with a lack of trust. I could not – or would not -- trust those three men with my own fragile feelings or the turmoil in my soul. I would not trust them to help me through the process. I could not trust them to accept me, not pity me nor look down on me. Like my mother I was struck dumb by my own choice. Like my mother I cut myself off from those who might have been willing to understand me.

So where in this story of self-imposed isolation are there glimpses of grace? Let me name three. First, I remember the gentle concern of my judge-turned-brother who spoke to me as I left the place of execution with my head under my arm. Second, I remember the silent listening and caring presence of my wife on the telephone. Finally, I recall the friend and mentor who reached out a hand to pull me up out of the waters of mistrust.

ON BEING AFRAID OF THE DARK

If I say, 'Let only darkness cover me and the light about me be night,' Even the darkness is not dark to Thee, the night is bright as the day; for darkness is as light with Thee.
Psalm 139

It was five years ago this week that we huddled in our homes at two a.m., listening to a roaring locomotive passing overhead, bringing trees crashing down in its wake. If you were not here on the night of Hurricane Fran, you have heard your neighbors tell about it. If you were here, you have not forgotten the sounds or the feelings. As someone said, those who claim they slept through it all are either lucky or lying.

I think it is safe to say that the hurricane was perhaps a little more frightening because it happened at night. It would have been scary to watch the rain and to see the trees come down, but I suspect that it was even scarier to look out of our blacked out homes into the even deeper blackness ... and wait ... and wonder. There is something frightening about darkness. Ancient peoples created festivals in midwinter to try to persuade the sun to come back and slow the darkness that seemed to eat up the daylight hours. Children – and many grown ups – find themselves lying in bed watching shadows and trying not to let their fears turn them into monsters. Those who have watched the death of a loved one have felt what they would call darkness descend on their hearts.

In one sense it is natural to be afraid of the dark. Darkness means many things in our thinking, most of them bad. Darkness means mystery, pain, sadness, death, evil. And yet darkness can also mean a time for rest, a relief from distraction, a meeting place for lovers, an invitation to prayer. Some people welcome darkness as young Juliet welcomed it when darkness meant the coming of her lover:

Come, gentle night. . . give me my Romeo; and when he shall die, take him and cut him out in little stars, and he will make the face of heaven so fine that all the world will be in love with night, and pay no worship to the garish sun.

Well, we may never "be in love with night." But I think we all are touched somewhere within ourselves by that song from *Carousel:* "When you walk through a storm, hold your head up high and don't be afraid of the dark." What is it about the dark that makes us afraid? How can the darkness be a friend to us? Is there a word for us today that can give us courage to embrace the darkness?

I

What is it about the dark that makes us fearful? When I have asked people this question I have heard variations on three answers. We are afraid of the unknown. We are afraid of our own worst fantasies. And we are afraid of being alone.

We are afraid of the unknown. In the dark we cannot see our next step. We cannot prepare ourselves for what may confront us. In the dark we have much less control over what may happen next, and so we find ourselves pleading, "Don't keep me in the dark." When we are aware of darkness in our house or in our minds or in our lives we are aware that we are surrounded by mystery. And living with mystery is not comfortable or secure, whether we are in the dark about our next step or our next day, our next job or our next relationship.

This points to a second reason for our fearfulness.

Someone said, "It seems that when we're in the dark we expect the worst to happen. We always seem to be looking for the bogeyman." It is true, I think, that *we are afraid of our own worst fantasies.* When I lay awake as a child watching that dark form in the corner of my bedroom, I was pretty sure it was an intruder waiting for me to sleep so that he could pounce. It did not occur to me that it might be a robe draped over a chair. Why do we expect the worst? Carl Jung would say that we are afraid of our own shadow, that we are projecting on those innocent dark chairs the threatening shadow side of ourselves. Could be. Could be that our fear of the dark has to do, at least in part, with our fear of the dark places in our own hearts that we would rather not expose to the light.

We are afraid of being alone. When we are in the dark we cannot see those upon whom we depend for companionship. We are, in a sense, all by ourselves. It is no accident that children want to take someone's hand when they are walking at night. It is no accident that when we enter a darkened house we want to call out, "anybody home?" If in the darkness I cannot see those whom I love, then I want to hear them or touch them. If my world is darkened by pain or grief or fear, I want to know that I am not alone.

II

A familiar song begins with these words: "Hello, darkness, my old friend." Can darkness be our friend? Can we find in darkness something of value? Let me name two ways that I believe that can happen.

First, *darkness can help us to see more clearly.* Does this sound strange? Well, one summer in Vermont a young friend of ours finally, at the age of twelve, got his first clear view of the Milky Way. It's not that the Milky Way is not always up there, even for those of us here in Cary. But there is usually too much light to see it clearly. The darkness of rural Vermont is really dark. There is no city glow to keep you from seeing the dazzling spectacle of a starry night. Perhaps there are other ways in which too much light keeps us from seeing clearly. Perhaps the dazzle of too many possessions keeps us from seeing what is most valuable in life. Perhaps the darkness of loss helps us to see more clearly how precious are the persons who touch our lives.

Second, *darkness can help us to understand others more deeply.* Have you ever tried to look through a window from a brightly lighted place into a dark room? You will see a lot of your own reflection, but very little of what is within the room. Perhaps it is equally hard to see into the dark places of another's heart when our own lives seem full of light. Most of us have discovered that those who best understand and feel for us in our sadness or fear or pain are those who have experienced some dark times of their own. We are called as brothers and sisters in God's family to be compassionate, to walk with those in darkness and somehow feel it with them. Another voice from the Psalms says that "deep calls unto deep." We could also say that darkness understands darkness

III

We have many reasons to fear the dark and yet somehow, if we are to see more clearly and understand more deeply, we must find the courage to enter into the dark. Is there a word for us to give us that courage? I believe that there is.

First, we need to remind ourselves that "dark" does not equal bad. Someone pointed out that the first chapter of Genesis tells us that God created the light and called it good. True enough. But calling the light good does not mean that we must call the darkness bad. We need to remind ourselves that half of our lives are lived in darkness. Without that darkness we would have a hard time sleeping. Prisoners are sometimes forced to live in a lighted cell twenty-four hours a day. My guess is that they would welcome darkness as an old friend. Darkness is not evil. Darkness is a part of God's good creation.

Second, we need somehow to trust that entering into the darkness does not carry us away from God. The Psalmist says that *"even the darkness is not dark to Thee."* That is, what we think of as darkness is simply another part of the dwelling place of God. It is as though we walked into a dark room where we felt afraid and disoriented and alone only to find that there was someone already there, someone whose eyes were accustomed to the dark, someone who could take our arm and accompany us. Yet another psalmist puts it this way: "even though I walk through the valley of the shadow of death, I will fear no evil, for Thou art with me."

There is no greater fear, I think, than the fear that we must face the difficulties of life or walk the passageway of death without being certain that God is with us. And yet the central symbol of our faith reminds us that there is literally no dark place, in life or death, that Christ has not visited before us. The song from *Carousel* reminds us: *Walk on, walk on with hope in your heart and you'll never walk alone. You'll never walk alone.*

WALKING ALONE

None of my daughters is what you would call a loner. All have a way with words, all enjoy good company. Because this is true, I have admired them even more for the times they chose, for very good reasons, to walk alone.

Jane's chance came when she was about fifteen. Our firstborn had gathered a circle of girl friends in the high school during her first year there. It had taken a while, since she had attended middle school in another town and knew no one in the new school. Then she introduced them, and us, to Mason. Mason was a gentle young man whose name and skin color spoke of his ancestors in slavery. We admired her for her open attitude, even while we feared for the social consequences she might suffer. Our admiration and our fears were both well founded. She did indeed "lose touch" with most of the circle of girl friends. She paid a heavy price over the next three years in the small world of small town Virginia. But she chose to walk alone rather than turn her back on a new friend. I learned something from Jane about moral courage.

Ellen had many good friends in both high school and college. Where her older sister had gone north to college, she chose to go south, wanting to make a place for herself where no one knew her talented sister. After college Ellen took a one year job that would send her across the country to three cities where she would teach learning skills in high schools. She traveled, with all her possessions in her little un-air-conditioned car, to Minneapolis, Salt Lake City and Tucson. It was in Salt Lake City that she chose to walk alone. The family with whom she had a room was away for

Thanksgiving. After helping at a soup kitchen on Thursday, she still had a three day weekend to spend alone. She drove hours to Canyonlands National Park and sat where she could take in the view. It was, she told us later, as if she were the only human being in all that vastness. Rather than seek some kind of temporary comfort with strangers in a mall or movie – or even church – she chose to walk alone in a solitary place. I learned something from Ellen about making friends with oneself in solitude.

Kate's choice came in connection with church. Our youngest daughter had often chosen her own path in ways that made the family hold its breath. Since I had been organizing pastor of the little Presbyterian church in which the family grew up, it seemed likely that all three daughters would attend church, Sunday School, youth group and, at about 12 or 13, go through the process called confirmation. Wrong. Kate boycotted (girlcotted?) all of the above (although she did accompany me on Sunday mornings when I preached in other towns). In the face of family tradition and church expectation, she chose to walk alone. Over the years it has become clear that Kate had, and still has, a deeply spiritual side that has often not found expression in the traditional language of mainstream Protestantism. Rather than mouth words that she did not believe, she chose to walk alone. From Kate I have learned to respect those who walk to a different drummer.

TROUBLED WATERS

When you pass through the waters I will be with you; and through the rivers they shall not overwhelm you.

Isaiah 43:2

The Bible is full of stories in which water is a place of danger. Think of Noah and the flood, Moses and the Red Sea, Jonah and the whale, the disciples and the storm on Galilee, Paul's shipwreck. Just thinking about all these stories brings to my mind a bit of verse I heard somewhere. It goes something like this:

"Father, dear Father, may I go for a swim?" "Yes, my darling daughter. Just hang your clothes on a hickory limb. But don't go near the water." But if we think that way, we learn very quickly that that is not God's way with us, or our way with one another. We have to go near the water. And if we don't, the water is probably going to come near to us.

Have you ever tried to stay away from the dangerous waters of life? What happens? Suppose, by reason of caution or pickiness, you manage to avoid the stormy waters of intimate relationships. Eventually you find yourself sinking in the still waters of loneliness.

Suppose, by reason of good genes, good habits and good luck you steer clear of the chilly waters of illness or accident. Sooner or later you will find yourself in the even chillier waters of aging and gradual disability.

Maybe by reason of temperament or Prozac you are spared the deep waters of depression; you may yet feel stranded in the shallow waters of boredom. Maybe hard work and fortunate birth allow you to live your life safe from the dark waters of poverty; you will find that no amount of wealth can spare you the floods of grief when you lose someone you love.

As far as I can tell there is no way not to go near the water. And sometimes it seems that the waters are in fact going to be too much for us to survive. So think with me about some of the dangers that wait for us; about how God comes to us when we pass through the waters; about how we come to each other.

I

What are some of the dangers that wait for us on the water, dangers that sometimes threaten to overwhelm us?

Well, sometimes the threat is from the winds that seem to throw us about. They may be literal storms that flood our homes and knock down power lines, or storms of war that tear apart nations and destroy cities and rob families of loved ones. Some of the winds are felt within our own home – winds of marital conflict; or even in our church family – winds of disagreement and resentment. Sometimes the winds seem so strong that we are not at all sure that our little boats will ride out the storm.

Sometimes the waters are troubled by threats that lie beneath the surface. In the lake near my home the parents of the newborn ducklings try each spring to keep their tiny offspring alive until they are big enough to survive the snapping turtles that pull them under. As I watch from the shore and root for the ducklings, I think about the snapping turtles that threaten to pull us under. Some of the snapping turtles are within us, like the cancers that may grow in our bodies without our knowledge or mental illness that no one else sees but that pulls at us all the time. Some of the snapping turtles are of the human variety: violent turtles that make us feel uneasy on our city streets at night, and white collar turtles that drain us as a society and violate our environment while growing fat with obscene riches.

Sometimes the water itself is a threat, simply because of its width or depth. There are depths that we think will surely sink us, depths of shame, grief, disappointment, depression – depths that we alone know, that even those close to us do not see unless we let them see beneath the surface. And then there are times when the waters just seem too wide to get across, when we just get tired of swimming, or paddling, or waiting for a favorable wind.

II

How does God come to us on our troubled waters? We think of Noah, who was told to build a boat; Moses, who was chosen to lead his people through the swamps; Jesus, who joined his disciples in the middle of a storm. It seems that we can say two things about God's way with us on the water.

First, God does not take us out of the water but through it. Isaiah's word puts it simply: When you pass through the waters they will not overwhelm you. I have found nothing in the biblical tradition that suggests that God is likely to swoop down and rescue us from the waters…and much to suggest just the opposite. No matter how much we long for divine intervention, what God offers is divine presence. Jesus does not take his disciples out of the boat, he simply gets in the boat with them.

Second, God's way with us involves other people. Noah and Moses were God's agents in helping his people through the deep waters. Jesus in his very being is the one who bridges the gap between God and his frightened human children. God's promise is to be with us when we pass through the waters. But the bridges and the boats are going to be built by other human beings.

III

How then does God come to us in our troubled waters? Through the bridges we build to and for one another.

I was going to call this sermon "The Gospel According to Garfunkel," until I discovered that it was his partner Paul Simon who wrote the words of one of my favorite songs. Most of you are old enough to remember it. For those of you who are not, let me tell you how it goes:

When you're weary and feeling small, when tears are in your eyes, I will dry them all; I'm on your side. When times are tough and friends just can't be found, like a bridge over troubled waters I will lay me down.

When you're down and out, when you're on the street, when evening falls so hard, I will comfort you; I'll take your part. When darkness comes and pain is all around, like a bridge over troubled waters I will lay me down.

Just as Jesus is a bridge for us, restoring us to a sense of God's presence when we feel alone and afraid, so we can be a bridge to one another. And the kind of bridge we build will depend on the kind of troubled waters we find.

Some folk around us may be victims of flood waters that have wiped out their homes or the slow eroding waters of poverty that sap away their foundations. They may need very practical bridges of bricks and mortar, stone and steel, the kind that are built with dollars and labor, taxes and contributions, Habitat for Humanity or the Appalachian Service Project. Some of you are good at building that kind of bridge.

Other neighbors may be drowning in other kinds of waters. Right in our community there are immigrants or homegrown Americans who can't read, who are sinking in a sea of words they can't understand. They need a bridge of literacy that you can help build. There are children who have been neglected, elderly persons who can't afford their medicine. These brothers and sisters are struggling to stay afloat. They need a bridge of advocacy. Some of you can take the lead in fighting battles with government and other powerful interests, battles that these folk cannot fight for themselves.

Many people we meet every day are simply trying to survive the troubled waters of grief, disappointment, loneliness, unemployment, depression, divorce. The bridge they need most may be simply a bridge of understanding. Stephen Ministers build this kind of bridge for those who are trying to put their lives back together after a storm. The bridge may be built by a phone call, a cup of coffee, a note, a hand on the shoulder for someone who is being tugged at by the snapping turtles or drowning in the deep waters of despair. A bridge of understanding may literally be a bridge to new life.

The last part of the song gives a name to the kind of bridge that each one of us can be to our neighbors when they are in deep water. *Sail on silver girl, sail on by. Your time has come to shine; all your dreams are on their way. See how they shine! If you need a friend, I'm sailing right behind. Like a bridge over troubled waters I will ease your mind.* When things are going badly or even when it seems our time has come to shine – wherever our waters take us – we all need to know that there is someone sailing right behind. Jesus did not take his friends out of the storm; he joined them in the boat. We cannot protect one another from winds or storms, from depths or waves or snapping turtles. But we can sail alongside.

Keep these words in mind as you leave this place. Let them be your words, your promise to those whose lives you touch – as a Christian, as a brother or sister in faith, simply as a fellow human being who has been through some deep waters yourself. Call it a bridge of compassion, a bridge of love, or, simply, a bridge of friendship.

I think there is no one here so self-sufficient that he can say, "I don't need a friend." And I am sure that there is no one here so limited, so lacking in gifts, that she can say, "I cannot be a friend."

SIEGFRIED MEETS FATHER GOOSE

On the lake near my home I watched a dramatic and touching encounter between two beautiful and brave adversaries. Most satisfying to me was the fact that no one was hurt and that all parties left the field with a sense of satisfaction. It was, I think, what we humans would call a win-win conclusion.

Siegfried, a large male swan who has long been recognized as the patriarch of the lake, is known in the springtime to protect that part of the lakeshore where his current inamorata (probably one of his recent offspring) is nesting. Walkers along this part of the shore have learned to tread carefully, to push Siegfried gently away with long sticks, or even to turn and circle the lake in the other direction. Today the patriarch cruised in calm majesty just offshore near the nest.

As it happened, a pair of Canada geese were carefully tending their six fuzzy goslings on the path not too far beyond Siegfried's self-declared territory. They were, let it be clear, minding their own business. Unfortunately, a walker with a large black Lab approached the family of eight geese, so that both parents quickly shepherded their charges into the water and out of harm's way.

Apparently, a line in the water had been crossed, at least in Siegfried's mind. The black Lab had scarcely passed by when Siegfried approached the family of invaders, making a wake with the vigor of his rapid advance. The male adult, whom we shall call Father Goose, swam to meet him, making a naval battle imminent. Which would prevail – the big white protector of territory or the smaller bird swimming out to defend his brood?

What unfolded was a fascinating water chess game of move and countermove. Just before their courses collided, Father Goose veered off toward the center of the lake. Siegfried veered off in pursuit. As it seemed the powerfully-built swan would overtake the Canada goose, the smaller bird flapped his wings three or four times to move out of reach, then resumed swimming. Siegfried seemed ready to close the gap. This pattern of almost flight was repeated a half-dozen times, the two birds moving as though connected by an invisible rubber band.

At the far side of the lake, several hundred feet removed from both swan's nest and goslings, the battle ended suddenly without a shot being fired. Siegfried stopped his pursuit and watched as Father Goose swam safely away. The big swan stretched himself high out of the water, flapping his big, white wings in an unmistakable gesture of triumph. A few moments later, after giving his adversary time to crow, Father Goose spread his healthy wings and flew back across the lake to his little family, honking his delight as he landed.

The flapping of Siegfried seemed to be his way of announcing to the world, "Look at how I drove him away!" The honking of Father Goose seemed just as clearly his way of bragging to the family, "Look how I led him away!" Both birds had done their duty as protectors; both had saved their dignity as well as their feathers. Siegfried could take pride in his intimidating presence, Father Goose in his dramatic skills and his guile.

One question remains. While it is obvious that Father Goose could have flown away from the bigger bird, it is also obvious that such a flight would have defeated his purpose, since it would have left Siegfried too close to his unguarded family. It is not as obvious why Siegfried went along with the charade. Was he so dumb as to think that

Father Goose was really crippled and that a few more strong strokes would close the gap? Why was he hesitant to use his own big wings to help him pounce upon his fleeing adversary?

Siegfried knew, as Father Goose probably did not, that the big swan's wings were clipped, so that at best he could muster a strenuous and noisy flapping along the surface. My guess is that he chose to spare himself the indignity of being exposed as flightless, and so stayed in the water where he cut a more formidable figure. Or could it be that he knew something that we, his human cousins, tend to forget? I like to think that Siegfried somehow understood that success without violence is better than success with violence, which may in fact turn out to be no success at all.

THE REAL WORLD

I have seen that the race is not always to the swift, nor bread to the wise, nor favor to men of skill . . . but time and chance happen to them all.

Ecclesiastes 9:11

Watching the demonstrations on the streets of Beirut and then seeing the bloodshed on the streets of Baghdad makes the story of Palm Sunday strangely familiar. Now as then men and women take to the streets to celebrate a glimmer of hope and demonstrate for anyone who seems to offer a new start. Then, as now, once-hopeful crowds find themselves grieving the violent death of their dreams of peace.

Palm Sunday is a day for cynics to smile knowingly and optimists to shake their heads, a day when we are reminded once again that the real world is full of sweet beginnings followed by bitter endings. Some years ago when our youngest daughter was eighteen, her grandmother was speaking unhappily about how someone dear to her had done something that disappointed her. Kate shrugged and replied with a slightly laundered version of a current bumper sticker. "Oh well," she said, "it happens."

Yes, indeed. The real world is a place where "it happens." Alzheimer's happens, and addiction, and autism. But the real world is also the place where Beethoven happens, and butterflies. Tsunamis happen, so do daffodils. Hitler happens in the real world, but so does Gandhi. Good Friday happens, and also Easter. Palm Sunday reminds us that the real world is a place where "it happens" because today we can see the clouds gathering on the same day as the parade. The real world, then, is the world described with such relentless candor by the Preacher, a world where the race is not always to the swift nor the battle to the strong, nor bread to the wise, nor riches to the intelligent, nor favor to the men of skill. It is a world where time and chance happen to them all.

So we speak about Palm Sunday with a certain sadness or with a certain grim humor. Because reality is sometimes grim. Reality insists on reminding us that we are limited creatures whose ideals and hopes exceed our capacities; that our physical power will diminish as our understanding increases; that we will suffer as many defeats as victories; that many things that happen will not make much sense to us; that we have only limited ability to protect either ourselves or those we love from harm. The reality is that life will be sometimes unfair, often difficult, always a perplexing mix of beauty and ugliness, cruelty and compassion, sincerity and sham, evil and good.

If this is indeed the real world, this place where time and chance happen to us all, then we have an important choice to make, a choice about how we shall live in the real world. The choice we have is not *whether* we will face hurt, disappointment and loss, but about *how* we will face them when they come. The control we have is not control over what happens to us or our loved ones but over how we respond to what happens.

How, then, will we choose to live in the real world? Let me name four options that we can choose when we are confronted with the hard happenings of the real world. Each of us has, at one time or another, chosen all of them. But the way we choose to live most of the time, the way we typically respond to the real world, will color who we are and who we become.

I

We may choose to reject the real world. That is, we may find ways to shut out those parts of life that are too hard to face. Like Scarlett O'Hara we may decide to "think about it tomorrow." Like a father whose teenage son died tragically, we may choose to "take our grief in little bites." We may concentrate our attention on some small part of reality that is more or less under control to keep from feeling overwhelmed by too much reality.

All of us pretend sometimes. All of us need, sometimes, to pretend. Denial is a necessary device that helps us limit ourselves to as much reality as we feel we can handle, to take reality, if you will, in little bites. But we may get in the habit of rejecting the real world in a systematic way. We may avoid looking at the unpleasant stories in the daily paper; we may numb ourselves with alcohol or television or shopping. We may even use religion this way, focusing on our "spiritual life" or on "the next life" so that we can tune out the hardness of life around us. (Which may be why religion has sometimes been called an "opiate.")

But if I read the gospels correctly, the Jesus I see there was one who wept over Jerusalem, confronted injustice and hypocrisy where he found it, felt pain and thirst and grief. This Jesus was not one who rejected the real world in which he lived.

II

We may choose to resent the real world. Of course we get angry at injustice. We complain when suffering seems to fall unevenly and even unfairly on those who do not deserve it. There is plenty of reason to get angry at the real world. But we may make it more than a feeling or a response. We may make anger a refrain, telling the world that life isn't fair, collecting grievances, placing blame, nursing grudges, planning revenge. Anger may, in a word, become a habit that we feed.

Those who resent the real world may become persistently angry about what life has done to them or to their loved ones. Sad to say, what life has done to them is not nearly as bad as what they are doing to themselves. If we give more attention to the suffering of life than it deserves, if "life isn't fair" becomes our motto, then we will simply add to the unavoidable pain of life a dark layer of bitterness. Someone has said it this way: "suffering is inevitable; misery is an option."

III

We may choose to endure the real world. Our refrain will not be "life is unfair" but "life is difficult." A certain Scott Peck began his bestselling book with these arresting words. We will be sad rather than cynical about the sorrows of life. Our attitude will be closer to resignation than bitterness. This is an attitude that has a certain willingness to accept the hard realities of the world. It is realistic to feel sad about the hurts and disappointments of life. Anyone who can watch the nightly news without feeling sad about the suffering of fellow humans around the world is lacking in imagination or compassion or both. Realizing that "life is difficult" is not a bad way to get your perspective on the real world. It is certainly better than "life is not real" or "life is bad." Many people of faith see the hardships of the real world as a test of endurance and even explain their difficulties as a part of the system, as though God built in a few obstacles to improve our character.

It does not seem to me that Jesus sees the hardships of life as God-given obstacles. Certainly he does not excuse human evil that way. It seems to me that Jesus looks at sickness and poverty and injustice as a part of life but not as God's purpose for life. To choose to endure the real world is to train ourselves to a kind of stoic resilience which takes a lot of courage and acceptance and even a grim sense of humor. It may also mean that we miss some opportunities for joy.

IV

We may choose to embrace the real world. Rather than "life is unreal" or "life is unfair" or even "life is difficult," we may look at the real world with our eyes open and see that it is both good and bad, beautiful and bleak, full of possibilities for both suffering and joy. What does it mean to embrace the real world? Let me share what it means to me.

To embrace the real world means giving suffering its due but not more than its due. After all, if we are going to allow ourselves to love anyone we are going to suffer with them and for them. We are going to expose ourselves to disappointment, hurt, conflict and grief simply by letting others be important to us. But who would say that the chance to love is not worth the suffering? To embrace the real world means taking on the difficulties of life as an opportunity to make that world, or at least our little corner of it, a little better than we found it. To embrace the real world means accepting the unfairness and the hardness and still believing that somehow it is all worth it, that at the heart of things is a loving Spirit with a good and loving purpose.

And that takes an act of faith. On Palm Sunday we stand alongside those who welcomed to Jerusalem the one who came to give their lives meaning, knowing, *as they did not know,* that before the week was out the real world would do its worst to him, and believing that he, by embracing the real world, would overcome that worst with his best.

Palm Sunday is a day for embracing the real world. We sing hymns celebrating God's goodness in the very shadow of the cross that put goodness to death. We wave our branches knowing that the real world is a world full of shadows – shadows cast by time and by chance and by human failure, including our own. It really is all about attitude. It takes faith and courage to embrace that world as it is – to accept it, to love it, to try to leave it a little better.

WHAT WE WISH FOR

Jackie Marshall was a liberated woman long before most women had discovered that they were indentured. Whether by choice or necessity she was a single schoolteacher to whom the label "old maid" would not naturally apply. She wrote poetry, some of it very funny. She told stories of questionable taste and taught her class in creative writing with fervor, flair and sometimes frankly odd pedagogic tools.

For example, she felt that an excellent way to absorb the literary style of an admired master was to copy his work until his way with words had somehow sunk in. Copy, not imitate. Word by word by word. It was in this fashion that I was introduced to "The Cask of Amontillado." I was, Miss Marshall informed me, to copy Poe's story five times. Verbatim. By hand. I would, she assured me, find myself a better writer for the experience. She believed, apparently, that Poe's genius would somehow make its way up my writing arm and into my bones, my mind, perhaps my very soul.

I was more than skeptical. I was horrified. Not only did I dread the drudgery, I could see no way that such robotic labor could set me free to creative flights (although I now suspect that freedom was not the only thing she had in mind). But I was also a little afraid of this outspoken and unconventional woman. She had a piercing look and a tilt to her chin that suggested she welcomed a good fight. Besides, she seemed to be grooming me to edit a new literary magazine and I did not want to ruin my chances by quarreling with her. So I sat down to write.

"The thousand injuries of Fortunato I had borne as best I could." As we made our way slowly down the steps of the wine cellar I flipped the pages more and more often to measure my progress, like a child on a long trip who whines from the back seat, "Are we there yet?" I resented Poe's every superfluous word. I fervently wished him to get to the point. I took little joy in the slowly dawning terror of Fortunato as he realized his fate. By the time I had completed my first copy, exhausted and resentful, I longed like Fortunato for escape from this cramped writer's prison.

I will not say that I prayed for a way out. My strictly Presbyterian theology would not allow me, even at eighteen, to ask God to get me out of work. But I did devoutly wish that something would come up to get me off this wearisome hook. And something did. As I drove home from the library on the very next day, I was struck by a sharp pain in the chest, so sharp that I could not turn the steering wheel without gasping. I pulled the car to the curb and sat, shaking. My first thought was, "I'm having a heart attack and I'm so young." A second thought tumbled out; "I won't have to write any more copies." Somewhat later a third, more considered thought arrived: "If I live through this, I will be more careful what I wish for."

The divine intervention worked. Our family doctor officially pronounced me victim of the suitably impressive illness called pleurisy and advised me to languish in bed for a week. When I returned to Miss Marshall's class she took one look at her pale editor-to-be and said that perhaps I should skip the copying assignment. Apparently she valued her infant literary magazine (and perhaps my health) more than her crazy pedagogic theory.

I have always felt slightly guilty about my dramatic escape, as well as awed by the power of mind over body that produced such a perfect ailment on cue. Even then I *knew that both my health and my integrity would have been better served had I taken on Miss Marshall in a more straightforward fashion. I have sometimes wondered whether her piercing eye saw through my convenient crisis.*

I have also thought with satisfaction that I was more successful in my escape than poor Fortunato.

PUT TO THE TEST

Because he himself was tested by what he suffered, he is able to help those who are being tested.
Hebrews 2:18

It may seem strange that the lectionary reading for the first Sunday after Christmas should dwell on the suffering of Jesus. After all, we just finished hearing about his birth in all its simple beauty. It would be nice to relish the time of good tidings and peace on earth before we are forced to refocus on the bad tidings of war on earth.

But the readings for this day are actually a rather helpful reminder that the hardships that Jesus suffered were not confined to the last few days of his life. In his infancy his family had to flee from what we might today call "state sponsored terrorism." The gospel account of Herod reminds us of that terrible ancient massacre that sounds all too modern – what is referred to as the slaughter of the innocents. Of course Jesus did not know of it at the time, but you have to wonder how he felt later on when he learned that many baby boys died as a result of his birth. At any rate, because of Herod's paranoid rage, Jesus' parents spent two years in Egypt. The child spent his first years as a refugee and his whole life in a land ruled by foreigners who kept the native Jewish population under tight, humiliating control. Again, it sounds like modern Palestine, except that the power is now in the hands of Jews.

Jesus grew up in the family of a tradesman, one of a class which was treated in that time as "marginal." And just as he probably heard about the murders committed by

Herod at the time of his birth, he also certainly lived with rumors about his own paternity. It was whispered that Joseph was not his father, which made Jesus "marginal" in more ways than one. By the time he was a young man Jesus had already struggled with many painful questions about his identity and many moments of feeling like an outsider. No wonder he was able to identify so readily with the poor, the outcasts, the mentally ill, the children and women and foreigners who were treated by those in power as less than human.

The writer says that he was "tested by suffering." We usually think of that test as the one that came in Jerusalem many years later, when Jesus chose at the risk of his life to be faithful to his understanding of God's will for his life. But what about the other kinds of suffering that came as a part of just being human? Weren't they tests as well?

What is the difference between a test and a temptation? When we pray "lead us not into temptation," are we really thinking and hoping that we will not be put to the test? It seems to me that every experience of life is a test – the difficult ones, certainly, but even those experiences that might seem to be easy or even pleasant. How does a test become a temptation? Well, think of it this way. Every difficult experience may be seen as a challenge to grow as a human being or it may be an opportunity to cop out or to cheat. As a good friend of mine put it, each test is also a temptation to self-indulgence.

When I was going to youth group as a teenager, we sang a song called "Yield Not to Temptation." One especially memorable line went like this: "fight manfully onward, dark passions subdue." I don't know how well I did at fighting manfully onward, but my imagination was certainly stirred by those words about "dark passions." Oscar Wilde once said, "I can resist everything but temptation." The opportunity for self-indulgence is always there, and always tempting. What are some of the ways we are tested, challenged and tempted?

The most familiar form of test is the one that comes on a piece of paper. The challenge is to answer the questions honestly and to the best of our ability, to see that we are being tested for our competence and our integrity. The temptation, of course, is to cheat – by using forbidden materials or to cop out by refusing to do our best.

Financial insecurity is a test. The temptation in such a time is to become tightfisted, even greedy. The challenge is to keep our minds and hearts and wallets open to those who depend on us or those who are less secure than we. All of us are facing that test right now as we wrestle with our priorities for the new year to come.

Boredom is a test. When we are bored we are tempted to do things to excess to try to make life more interesting. So we may drink too much, spend too much, stretch too far the boundaries of marital fidelity. The challenge of boredom is to find creative ways to recover meaning for our lives rather than settling for shortcuts.

Being hurt by someone is a test. We are tempted to look for an opportunity for revenge, in the meantime "nursing our grudge to keep it warm," as Robert Burns said. The challenge when we are hurt is to learn how to see the person who hurt us as another struggling human being and not simply an enemy. The challenge is to discover how to forgive.

Sickness is definitely a test. When we are sick or hurt we are tempted to succumb to the luxury of self-pity and to hope that others will pity us as well. The challenge is to make the best of our limitations, do what we can for our woundedness, and in the process maybe learn something about compassion for others who suffer.

It occurs to me that *we are tested even by prosperity.* When things are going well for us, the temptation is to believe that we are somehow entitled to more of the same, so that we complain when times are less prosperous. What is the challenge? The challenge, it seems to me, is to find in our times of prosperity an opportunity for gratitude and generosity.

Finally, of course, *we are tested by conflict.* In times of conflict, between husbands and wives or parents and children, between nations or ethnic groups, the temptation we all face is the temptation to pretend to ourselves that we hold the moral high ground. The challenge for us is to be honest about the part we have played bringing the conflict about, instead of reducing every conflict to a battle between good (us) and evil (them).

Americans are being tested right now. And the jury is still out on how we rise to the challenges that have faced us since September 11. Those first terrible days seemed to bring out the best in us: in the heroism of rescue workers; the generosity of those who gave blood, money, food; the prayers of thousands more who poured out their hearts for the victims and their longing for peace and understanding.

What the long months and years will bring out in us remains to be seen. Can we survive terrorism without becoming terrorists? Can we be targets of hatred without being infected by hatred? Can we protect our land and our children without closing minds and hearts to those in other lands whose children suffer? Can we continue to pay attention to the needs of the "least of our brothers and sisters" – the poor, the very young, the elderly sick? Can we find within ourselves the resources and the will to respond to them as quickly and as generously as we respond to demands for arms? The jury, I would say, is still out.

So what are we asking when we pray "lead us not into temptation"? Surely we cannot ask that we not be tested. And surely the one who taught us this prayer, tested as he was by a lifetime of suffering, knew that testing is simply a part of being human. I think that Jesus meant something like this: "When life puts us to the test, help us to face it without giving in to temptation; deliver us from the worst within us that is always tempting us to give up on the best that is in us."

There is a good New Year's word for us as we prepare for a new round of testing. The one who taught us that prayer has been put to every test that we have faced or will face. He knows how it feels to be an outsider, suffer injustice, endure poverty, live with oppression, feel the pain of betrayal. When we are put to the test, as surely we will be, we can know that there is one like us who has been there before. He cannot take our tests for us. But he will and does walk by our side.

HOW I LEARNED ABOUT MENDACITY

It was Big Daddy, the shrewd southern papa in *Cat on a Hot Tin Roof*, who taught me the word. "Mendacity," Burl Ives would drawl with his frightening smile, "I could write a book on it and still not cover the subject." I learned the word from Big Daddy, but I had already smelled it without knowing its name. My most memorable whiff of mendacity came when I was about ten years old. The smell lingers.

 I didn't really like Bobby, even though we spent a lot of time together as playmates. He lived next door and he had a lot of toys. This happy combination of proximity and treasure touched me at my most vulnerable point and successfully tempted me to overcome my aversion to the owner of the toys and keep him company in the playroom that was attached to his family's garage. I thought privately that he was a spoiled brat indulged by his parents with far too much stuff. I even guessed (or heard my mother guess) that the abundance of toys was his parents' way of consoling him as the neighborhood outcast. I also suspected that his stable of treats had been created for the purpose of luring kids like me into playing with this obnoxious child. Whether this last suspicion was an accurate reading of our neighbors' intentions, it was certainly an accurate reading of the result. The lure worked. I spent many hours with Bobby, selling my condescending companionship for a mess of his possessions.

 I don't know whether Bobby ever detected my dislike for him. I preferred to think that he was too dense and too self-centered to notice. Or that I was too smooth (not to mention decent) to let my true feelings show. As I reflect on my encounter with the full hostile force of his mendacity, I wonder whether he was as dense as I supposed him to be and whether my own deceit was as well disguised as I imagined.

It was in a brief throwaway moment that I first smelled the smell. We were playing in his front yard in the late afternoon. For some reason I was holding a dead branch in one hand, a crooked stick about the size of a misshapen yardstick. Bobby and I were arguing about something, a normal sort of thing between us and not even particularly heated at that. We were at a standstill, glaring at each other in frustration, when Bobby's mother came out of her house and called from the front porch, "What's going on out there?" Without taking his eyes off me, Bobby answered his mother in a matter-of-fact tone, "David just hit me with that stick." I am sure that my face was a study in shock and outraged innocence. I was quite literally rendered speechless by the sheer audacity of his lie. We were too far from the porch for Bobby's mother to see him grin at me – a grin of triumph. There was no doubt that he had won. Nothing I could say would sound right. Worse, there was no chance that I could successfully make my case to Bobby's favorite protector. What could I say, "Mrs. Goodwin, your son is a liar?"

There was a long silent moment during which Bobby grinned, Mrs. Goodwin looked troubled, and I stared in disbelief at this shameless perpetrator of what I would later come to recognize as the Big Lie. His mother broke the silence. "Well, you'd better come on in the house to supper", she said, obviously concluding that she must remove her child from the vicious presence of this next door barbarian. Bobby smirked at me as he walked away. In my embarrassment and outrage, I felt a sudden urge to break the stick over the head of my smug enemy and thus *confirm in his mother's mind the low opinion she was already forming of me. But my arm worked no better than my tongue. I stood, stick in hand, and watched him go.*

Many years had to pass before I could think beyond my wounded innocence to the words of Big Daddy. "Pretense! Ain't that mendacity? Having to pretend stuff you don't think or feel." My encounter with Bobby's flagrant use of the Big Lie was so stunning that it blinded me to the more subtly mendacious pretense I had practiced in my daily visits to his playroom. Perhaps his crude accusation worked so well on that long ago afternoon because I found myself not only disarmed, but unmasked. Mendacity comes in many shapes, big lies and pretense being two of them. But the smell is the same.

SOLIDARITY

It was fitting that God, for whom and through whom all things exist . . . should make the pioneer of their salvation perfect through suffering.

Hebrews 2:10

Some twenty years ago our newscasts told us of an amazing underground movement that burst into view, leading to the first major break in the Soviet domination of Eastern Europe and the first step in the ending of the Cold War. Suddenly we in the West became aware of a powerful non-violent revolution that overthrew the communist government of Poland. The image I remember most was a flag with a single word. Even I could translate it into English. The word was Solidarity. Solidarity. A powerful word that gives a name to that sense of unity we feel when we are drawn together in common cause. I want to ask you to think about the kinds of solidarity we experience – and a kind that we need to experience.

There is the solidarity we feel in times of crisis. Whether the crisis is caused by terrorists or by hurricanes we all have seen communities bond together to help each other. We have seen neighbors act like neighbors. We ourselves have been drawn out of our ordinary self-absorption into acts of helpfulness that extend even to strangers. Crisis is one of the magnets that draws us together in solidarity.

There is another magnet, somewhat similar to crisis, that creates a solidarity all of us know. Call it the *solidarity of suffering*. When Job suffers misfortune his friends gather to commiserate. When you and I experience some hurt or loss or injustice, we look around for someone with whom to share it. Some of you will remember Dr. Eric Berne, who wrote a bestseller some time back called *Games People Play*. One of the games he described that struck me as a favorite – then and now – was the game he called "Ain't It Awful." An unlimited number can play. All you need is a common enemy, a common grievance, an injustice or inconvenience about which to complain – terrorists, the cost of insurance, the weather, the government, the irresponsibility of today's teenagers – or today's children, today's workers, today's business executives, today's athletes. The possibilities, you see, are literally endless. The only qualification for playing Ain't it Awful is to feel that you are a victim. Then you have only to find others who share your victimhood to play the game. Then there are two things you can do with this newfound solidarity in suffering. You can form a support group or you can simply participate in what has been called the culture of complaint.

Support groups are usually valuable. They enable human beings who have been hurt to gather their resources for change. A support group for alcoholics can help persons feel less alone and give them encouragement as they struggle to make a new life. A support group for parents who have lost children to drunk driving can organize the community to change the law. Support groups offer a constructive way in which our solidarity in suffering can draw us together in healing and creative ways. They can even help us feel less like victims. But there are also groups, formal and informal, whose only purpose seems to be to reinforce our sense of grievance; to assure us that we have good reason to be angry. "Ain't it awful!" we cry. And our fellow sufferers say, "That's not all. Let me tell you about awful." That is the kind of solidarity that helps perpetuate our culture of complaint.

Walking to Wisdom

There is another magnet that is something like a support group with a difference. It is not created by common suffering but by some common flaw. It is not so much designed to bring about creative change as to reinforce those bad habits we are not quite willing to give up. These groups may be very small. They are not usually designated as support groups at all, but they are immensely popular just the same. Somewhat like the solidarity of suffering, there is the *solidarity of sinning*. I've been thinking about the Seven Deadly Sins – what they do to us and what we can do to counter them before they lead us into shipwreck. In thinking about sin lately, I've come to believe that we like to invent small private clubs to make ourselves feel better about those actions or attitudes about which we feel a little guilty, but not guilty enough to change. I think of it as a kind of buddy system for sinners.

For example, I can feel better about my gluttony if I overeat in the company of friends. I can feel less shame about my drinking if I have buddies who encourage me to have another. I can justify my anger if I join a group that is angry at all kinds of things – perhaps I can become a devotee of talk radio. We can have shopping buddies to help us justify our greed, locker room buddies with whom we can feed our appetite for dirty jokes. We can even cultivate high class buddies, whom we see as a cut above the rest in brains or class or money or even holiness, so that we can take pride in being a cut above as well.

The examples I have offered cover five of the seven deadly sins. Maybe you can think of others. I could not think of a buddy system for envy, since we are usually slightly embarrassed about being envious and tend to keep it to ourselves. And I can't imagine a group for those who suffer from sloth since the slothful don't have enough energy to get to a meeting or organize activities, and if they did show up they would probably find that everyone else stayed home.

So, we are drawn together by many magnets. Some of them bring out the best in us, some the worst. We are drawn together by common crisis that calls us out of ourselves and into caring for others. We are drawn to those who have felt the same pain as we have felt when life treats us badly and we want support, or at least company in our complaint. We are drawn together by the struggles we experience with some besetting sin; and so we want help, or at least comfort, in our struggle.

I can think of one more magnet that draws us, perhaps greater than all the others but certainly more difficult to live. When we come to a place of worship, when we hear a story of Jesus and take it to heart, when we respond to the invitation to come to the communion table, then we are being drawn by the call of the one who is our host, whose very life defines the meaning of the table.

The writer to the Hebrews tells us that Jesus is one who identifies with us – all of us – in our weaknesses and our failures. He says that Jesus was "made perfect in suffering." I think that the word "perfect" here means "complete", "perfected", totally identified with humanity in its pain. Jesus is one with us in suffering, not only as a victim of human injustice and blindness and cruelty, but also as one who suffers with us when we suffer. He is one with the child who suffers abuse, one with the person made homeless by war or hopeless by poverty. He suffers with and for those who live in mental darkness or chaos, or, even worse, with those who live in the moral darkness of indifference.

Jesus' suffering is not the same as the suffering of Job. Job's suffering has to do with what happens to Job. Jesus' suffering is the suffering that he experiences in caring for humanity. A better word might be compassion. It is to this companionship with those who suffer that we are called when we come to the table. We are not simply asking for God's healing for our own hurts but we are asking for the power to take on Christ's concern for the hurts of others.

World Communion Sunday is a day to remember what it means to share at the table in Christ's ministry of compassion to those who are hungry, torn by war, victims of abuse or neglect. It is a day to recall, to demonstrate, to act on what we may call our *solidarity of compassion*, when we are companions with Christ in caring for a wounded world.

In *The Secret Life of Bees,* we meet a woman named May who grieves deeply when she hears of the pain of others. As her sister explains it, May "doesn't have the protection the rest of us have. Everything just comes into her – all the suffering out there – and she feels as if it's happening to her." We learn that May had a twin sister named April. They were so close that May felt all her pain. And when April killed herself, says her sister, "It seemed like the world itself became May's twin sister."

If you are like me you find it hard to sustain for very long any solidarity with those who suffer. You may have trouble feeling compassion for that annoying neighbor or irritating relative, much less for faceless brothers and sisters on the other side of the world. If you are like me you sometimes numb yourself to the suffering of others. You may refuse to read the paper or watch the newscasts. You may insulate yourself with the kind of indifference that Elie Wiesel calls "the refuge of those without imagination." If this is as true for you as it is for me, then there is all the more reason for us to be drawn to this table where our numb spirits may be touched, awakened, taught by the spirit of him who suffers with us and for us all.

WHO WAS THAT MASKED MAN?

The Phantom of the Opera is back on Broadway drawing the same big crowds. The plot is a strange tale of a mysterious masked intruder who seems to be promoting one young opera singer by killing off her competition. What makes this show so appealing besides the great songs and the chandelier-smashing drama? Is it the unlikely story, the rather ordinary hero and heroine, the exotic setting? Perhaps. Or perhaps there is something – or rather someone – in the story who strikes a familiar chord in all of us. I suspect that we are all drawn to the sad, scary and lonely figure behind the mask. I suspect we all know something about hiding behind masks, afraid to be seen and yet hoping somehow to be known and accepted, in spite of the shadowy inner person that might drive people away.

The Phantom fears that his ugliness will repel the one he loves. So he hides behind a mask and keeps everyone at a distance with his threatening ways. Others who wore masks come to mind. The Lone Ranger wore one, though he did not seem to be hiding ugliness or evil. What need did he have for a mask? Did he feel the need to maintain his aloneness, to keep anyone from getting so close that they might see beneath his heroic image? And what of the Pharisees? Jesus called them "Mask Wearers," the literal meaning of the Greek word "hypocrite." Were they hiding as well? Were the Pharisees' masks of piety a way of keeping secret from others (and even from themselves) the self-centered, all too human creature within?

Carl Jung gave a name to the mask that we all wear. He called it our *persona,* the face we present to the world.

He also named that part of ourselves that we feel a need to keep hidden. His name for it was *shadow*. The Phantom, the Lone Ranger, the Pharisee all demonstrate in dramatic form what each of us knows first hand. They remind us how our masks protect us and at the same time encumber us, keeping others from knowing us as we are.

So what can we do? Well, we can cling to our masks. That means clinging to our loneliness and to the projections by which we tend to lay on others those parts of ourselves that we cannot or will not acknowledge. All of us have a way of finding enemies to hate instead of owning what seems most alien within us. Sometimes whole nations label some external threat with whom to be at war so that they can maintain their own mask of innocence. We can cling to our masks, hide from our own shadows, blame others for our own self-rejection and our fear of exposure.

Or we can find a way to make peace with the part of ourselves from which we have felt a need to hide. We can learn about forgiveness – for ourselves as well as others – so that even our shadow can come into the light. We can discover how to be a real person in a world of real persons and less set apart as Lone Ranger, Pharisee or Phantom.

Every pastor knows persons who seem to be struggling to keep in place their own personal masks. Every pastor also knows how hard it is to stay behind his or her own mask of Cheerfully Faithful Nice Person. All of us long for a chance to unmask. We can, sometimes, let God know who we are (since we suspect that God knows anyway). But we wish, just the same, that we could trust another human being to meet our shadow face to face and help us to make peace. Pastors know a lot about masks and shadows. So do pastoral counselors. Maybe it is time to come out of hiding.

A PATH OF POSSIBILITIES

Then Jesus was led up by the Spirit into the wilderness to be tested...
                                              Matthew 4:1

What comes to mind when you hear the word "test"? Did you think of "stress"? Doesn't it seem to you that the phrase "stress test" is redundant? For most of us the very thought of testing is enough to raise our stress level, whether it has to do with proving our knowledge or getting into college, driving a car or passing the bar, qualifying for a position or satisfying a physician. (You see, the very idea of testing is so stressful it makes me retreat into rhyme just to ease the tension.) All of us get anxious about tests. We even relive that anxiety sometimes with our recurring dreams of showing up for the final exam without having read the book. Testing brings to mind thoughts of judgment, disapproval, failure, disappointment.

And now we are in the season of Lent, hearing about the testing of Jesus, expecting to hear more about temptation and not giving in and repentance and confession. More stress.

Well, let me offer another way of thinking about it. What if? What if you were to think of testing as a chance to look in a mirror and discover where you are on your own path of possibilities? What if testing became an opportunity for reflection instead of recrimination, growth instead of guilt, new possibilities instead of old failures? Recently I found myself eagerly awaiting the results of a test. I wanted to find out where I stood on a certain path. So when the nurse called from the radiologist's office to tell me that my PSA count was "less than 0.1," I was very happy. (For those of you who aren't familiar with this bit of *esoterica*, 0.1 is really good). For me this useful medical mirror was reflecting a specific feature of my physical self and telling me that my path of possibilities, at least by that particular mirror, was very promising.

So let me invite you to think of self-testing as a mirror in which to look at your own path. Specifically, look at the three tests by which Jesus reflected on his path and use them to take measure of your own. As Matthew tells it, Jesus went off by himself to look in the mirror, to consider some of the directions he might choose. Try putting these three tests to yourself. Not in order to feel judged or guilty, but simply as mirrors in which you can see yourself a bit more clearly.

I

Call the first one the Bread Test. You remember, the tempter suggests that the hungry man turn stones into bread, and Jesus refuses. "Man does not," he says, "live by bread alone." The question of the Bread Test is this: how important a place do we give to material things?

Now bread is important, both for ourselves and for our families. Try going a long time without food and see whether you can think about anything else. The world is full of good things to enjoy; we are born into a material world to live out God's purposes. But how important to us is bread? Important enough to set ourselves apart from other human beings in order to get it? Important enough to hurt people or use people for the sake of bread?

Jesus puts material things in perspective. Humanity lives by bread, but not by bread alone. Bread – and houses and cars and computers and clothes and savings and all the other things we feel we simply cannot do without – these are all a part of life but they are not the whole of life. When we make our decisions primarily to protect our standard of living; when we are more interested in property rights than in human rights; when things become more important than people, then we may need to reflect on how we are doing with the Bread Test.

The Russian theologian Berdyaev puts it very sharply: "Bread for myself is a material question; bread for my neighbor is a spiritual question." I believe that bread for myself should in some way help me grow more concerned about bread for my neighbor. If it does not, then I may be falling short on the Bread Test.

II

Then there is the Power Test. Jesus is tempted with the promise of power if he will sell his soul to the devil – the original Faustian bargain. He answers, "Worship God; serve God alone." The question for each of us is this: how important to us is power in our world of values, and how do we use it?

Your first thought may be, "But I have no power; I'm an ordinary person; power is for the "powerful." That is not true. Everyone has power. Power is God's gift, the gift of energy that each of us is given. The Latin word *potens* reminds us of its meaning, and that is "the ability to do things." Power is the energy God gives us to make the world a better place for ourselves and also for our sisters and brothers. Power is a means, not an end in itself.

But sometimes we try to get extra power to feed our shaky self-esteem; sometimes we want power over people instead of power for people. Sometimes we think that power means control, "the ability to make other people do things." As a nation we seem to assume that our accumulation of power carries with it the right to make other people do things our way. But if control means more to us than compassion, if winning is more important than sharing, if power is something to possess instead of something to use for good, then we may be falling short on the Power Test.

III

Finally there is the Miracle Test. Jesus is challenged to jump off the temple so that God can catch him (thus proving that God exists in order to rescue God's favorites). Jesus doesn't bite. "You shall not put God to the test." The question for our private reflection: does our faith depend on some assumption that God will come to our rescue?

Of course we hope for safety for ourselves and those we love. Of course we pray for their well being. But expecting God to intervene for us is more like a faith in magic than a trust in God. When bad things happen in our lives, and they certainly will, we may find ourselves thinking that God must be absent if the longed for miracle doesn't happen. In *The Brothers Karamazov*, the Grand Inquisitor argues with Christ. He accuses Christ of giving people a burden of freedom too heavy to bear. "People don't want God," he says, "people want miracles." Sometimes it seems that way. Sometimes it seems that we don't want to accept the freedom that God gives us; we want a miracle worker to bail us out when we are in trouble.

But when we make our faith a part of a "bargain for blessings," like Jacob at Bethel, we are putting God to the test instead of ourselves. We are assuming that God exists to protect us on our terms rather than that we exist to grow as children of God. To the extent that our faith depends on a guarantee of miraculous intervention, to that extent we are may need to reflect on the Miracle Test.

IV

Well, what did your glance in the mirror show you? Yes, I felt about the same. But this experiment in testing was not primarily to make us feel guilty. It was simply a way of reflecting on our own path of possibilities, of thinking about who we are, how we are doing, what we value or overvalue or undervalue, what place our faith has in our lives.

So, if you feel you fell short on the Bread Test, maybe you can find ways to simplify your life, ways that would free you from so much worry about material things. If you fell short on the Power Test, if you realized that you were confusing power with dominion or control, maybe you can look at new possibilities within yourself to use your energy in creative ways – ways that don't have to do with control, that don't, as Elie Wiesel put it, turn your dream into someone else's nightmare. Finally, if you were uneasy about the Miracle Test, if it is hard to trust yourself to a God who does not intervene, maybe you can find a new path of possibility, one in which you trust that there is enough of the divine Spirit within you to face whatever life brings you with creativity and grace.

The path of possibilities is a hard one, a lonesome valley if you will. No one can walk it for you, because no one else has your unique gifts, your potential, your choices. No one can walk it for you. But we do not walk it alone. Jesus also walked this valley; he faced the same tests we face. His Spirit is with us and in us when we walk our own path of possibilities.

NECESSARY LOSSES

When my father and my mother forsake me, then the Lord will take me up.

Psalm 27

Nobody likes to lose. Losing hurts, no matter how often or how inevitable the loss. Whether we are losing a game or a gamble, a favorite pet or a favorite dream, a grandparent or a best friend, we never quite get used to it. Never.

And yet all of us have known losses, and most certainly we will know more. It is one of the most painful and most familiar of human experiences. It will happen to us, literally, as sure as we are born. Because it is painful, we sometimes try to ignore it until it slaps us in the face, and we almost always shrink from loss as though it were something bad like medicine. And yet we know that loss, like medicine, is sometimes a necessary part of life as well as a painful one. And we suspect, in our most honest inward self, that the way we deal with loss may have a bearing on the way we live our lives.

So think with me about necessary loss – a title that I borrow from a wise and thoughtful book by Judith Viorst. If you have not read it, I commend it to you. You will be a wiser human being for taking the trouble. Ms. Viorst describes all the losses that are a necessary and natural part of human life and growth – natural because they happen to everyone in the course of growing up and growing older; necessary because without them we would not grow up, but would remain stuck in dependency and illusion.

What do we need to lose in order to grow? How can

we make the best of our necessary losses?

Three things that we must lose if we are to become whole: our dependency, our resentments, our illusions.

I

We need to lose our dependency. If a mother carries her child too long in her arms, he will not learn to walk. If she continues to prepare his meals and put the spoon in his mouth, he will not learn to feed himself. If she keeps reminding him what he needs to do at every hour of the day, he will never learn to discipline himself to remember.

We all know these elementary facts of parenting. Young, inexperienced parents know it and walk slowly beside their toddler offering encouragement. Children know it and fiercely claim the right to "do it myself" when parents are too protective. And yet there is a part of both parents and children that finds this lesson hard to learn.

Parents don't easily give up protecting and reminding and feeding. They want to be sure their child is safe and well-fed and off to a good start in life. And children don't always like to give up their dependency, since in all of us there is a struggle between the wish to be on our own and the wish to be taken care of. Sometimes it's nice to have someone fix their meals and keep them on schedule and protect them from the consequences of their carefree ways.

I think we never completely get over these conflicting feelings about dependency. Parents may give more advice to their grown up children than they ask for, grownups of all ages may act passive or helpless in the hope that somebody will take over the job of Mama or Papa. There is a dependent child in all of us. Husbands still long for a wife/mother to pick up their dirty socks, and wives still dream of a husband/father who will make them feel secure and happy.

II

There is a second necessary loss. When we lose someone we have depended on, we are often angry. "How could Mother let me oversleep and be late for school?" "How could my friend move away and leave me alone?" "How could my husband get sick and leave me with the burden of supporting the family?" Along with our dependency, we must also let go of the resentment that comes with our loss.

There will be times when a man will mutter to himself about having to take care of things that someone once did for him, just as there are times when a young man may be resentful when a girl friend breaks up with him, or when a woman is irritated that her husband spends a lot of time at work instead of keeping her company. It is important to let go of grudges and disappointment, to see our losses as necessary losses, so that we can look for new possibilities instead of being mired down in resentment.

I had a beautiful friend who died at the age of ninety seven. In her last years she began to lose her eyesight – a necessary loss of her old age. Instead of wasting time lamenting what she could no longer see, she began to listen to recorded books. She told me how she enjoyed sitting back with her eyes closed, enjoying the luxury of having someone read to her. Beyond this, she entertained herself with a 95 year treasury of memories, reliving trips she had taken with those who were dear to her. She was not bitter about her lost vision. She had let go her disappointment along with her sight.

III

Finally, we must let go of our illusions. One of the

hardest things to lose is your favorite notion of the way things – or persons – ought to be. You may have a dream of a perfect spouse who will greet you warmly every evening just like on TV. You may have an image of an ideal friend, doctor, pastor who will always have the right word to make you feel good. You may cling to a cherished, hazy memory of a flawless family that never was, but that is supposed to be created in your home.

In the same way you may have a favorite self image that you hold onto for dear life, an image that keeps you from having to face your own darker feelings and your more self-serving ways. There is nothing unusual about such illusions. We all wish for the perfect spouse, the perfect parent, the perfect child. And we all, at least some of the time, deceive ourselves with illusions about our own virtue.

But it is very important to let go of such illusions, or we will not be able to come to terms with the real human beings who meet us or the real human being within. Many marriages are shattered on the rock of such illusions, with both partners angry and disappointed that their hopes for the perfect spouse were not met. Many families live with an extra portion of conflict because parents will not give up their demand for perfect kids, and kids will not forgive their parents for being human.

And all of us find ourselves down on ourselves because we are not ready to suffer the loss of our own favorite daydreams. "If I cannot be the person I was supposed to be," someone said, "then I feel like a nothing." The loss of our illusions is a necessary loss. Otherwise was can never accept others, or ourselves, as we are.

IV

So how do we do it? What can help us begin to let go

of our dependencies, our disappointments, our daydreams? Let me offer two answers.

First, we must be willing to grieve our losses instead of insisting on getting our own way. A lot of our clinging to old dependencies, old grudges, old illusions is nothing more than an unwillingness to accept reality, a stubborn wish to have it our way. And one of the hard lessons of life is simply this: you can't have it all; you can't win them all; you can only truly enjoy life as it is if you are willing to suffer the pain of letting go of life as you wished it to be.

A second answer. We must learn to trust that we will survive our losses and even be better for them. This means trusting God and trusting ourselves. It means saying with the psalmist, "When my father and my mother forsake me, then the Lord will take me up."

Jesus says, "It is to your advantage that I leave, for I will send a comforter, a companion, a counselor." What is he saying? Well, I believe that he is telling his friends – and that includes us – that when they no longer have him to depend on they will discover a new Spirit within themselves to guide and empower them. He is saying, I believe, that their loss is a necessary loss.

In fact, his promise was fulfilled. For the frightened disciples who lost their leader on Good Friday found within themselves, in a few short weeks, the wisdom and the courage to become leaders instead of followers. The transformation of those early Christians from timid, dependent learners to bold, inspired teachers is testimony to the outcome of their necessary loss. They lost their leader. But they gained his Spirit within themselves.

And so it is for us. When we lose those we depend on, we gain new confidence in ourselves. When we give up our resentments and our grudges we gain a new appreciation of what is left. When we let go of our illusions about others we gain the ability to accept and forgive and enjoy them for who they are. When we give up our own secret illusions about ourselves, we take another step on the road to self-acceptance. That is, I believe, an incredible gain to come from a necessary loss.

FELLOW TRAVELERS

I am a man; I count nothing human alien to me.
- Terence

I am a part of all that I have met;
Yet all experience is an arch wherethro'
Gleams that untravelled world, whose margin fades
Forever and forever when I move.
- Tennyson

Everyone is a moon, and has a dark side which
he never shows to anybody.
- Mark Twain

TWO MILESTONES

This is none other than the house of God, and this is the gate of heaven.
                              Genesis 28:17

I have seen God face to face and yet my life is preserved.
                              Genesis 32:30

Charles Kuralt wrote about interstate highways and about the unpaved country roads of Vermont. Since I have spent a good many hours on both, I was attentive to his words:
   On the unbending interstate you can see the future ahead of you, many, many miles ahead. On a dirt road, however, you can see something better than that. You can see the past.
   It strikes me that the two milestone events we have heard from the journey of Jacob give us something of that same contrast. In the vision of the ladder at Bethel, Jacob's eye is fixed on the future. The past he wants desperately to leave behind; his perspectives, his plans, even his promises to God are all made with an eye to the future.
   If God will be with me and will keep me in the way that I go, and will give me bread to eat and clothing to wear . . . then the Lord shall be my God, and this stone, which I have set up for a pillar, shall be God's house; and of all that you give me I will surely give one-tenth to you.
   In his second milestone event –wrestling with the angel at Peniel some twenty years later – Jacob is finally coming to terms with his past. He has again left behind a trail of trickery, this time in his dealings with his father-in-

law Laban. This time, however, he is approaching no open future but a terrifying confrontation with the past in the person of Esau, the brother he cheated long ago and from whom he is estranged. This time he is anxiously preparing to make amends. This time his visionary experience carries more of the quality of struggle than of promise.

Two milestones that speak to our own experience. The first has the flavor of commencement; the second sounds more like mid-life crisis. The first has overtones of hope and inspiration; the second of struggle and reconciliation. At each milestone Jacob asks important questions about his journey and makes important discoveries. At Bethel Jacob comes away with a vision and a promise; at Peniel he limps away with a blessing and a new name. Look with me if you will at these two milestones – briefly at Bethel, for its meaning is clearer, more carefully at a midnight wrestling match that may illumine your own.

I

As he sets out to find a family and a fortune, Jacob spends the night on the road with only a stone for a pillow. Considering the discomfort of his bed and the dirty dealings of his recent past, Jacob's dream is remarkably comforting and comfortable. A heavenly escalator is the way I imagined it when I heard this story as a child. Instant access to the man upstairs. Whatever discomfort we may have with this ancient "penthouse" image of heaven, the meaning of the dream is fairly clear, both to Jacob and to us.

"Surely," says Jacob, "the Lord is in this place and I didn't know it." Jacob is discovering something crucial that we all need to discover: that the gateway to heaven is wherever we stand. Not only in some holy place, like church, or some holy land, like Palestine; not only in some holy time, like Sunday, or Easter morning, or AD 33. But here, now, wherever and whenever we open our spiritual eyes and hearts and pay attention. There is, as it were, an ongoing conversation between our world and the spirit world, an open line linking us to a divine power and presence. The image of the ladder is important, I think. It suggests something that is not permanent but portable. This gateway moves with us wherever we go. It is not a place to which we go, but a presence that goes with us. It is not something for Jacob, or us, to climb (despite the song) but something by which the divine comes down to accompany us on our way.

So – Jacob at Bethel is a lot like you and me: trying to outdistance our past rather than redeem it; bargaining with God for a long and happy life; building shrines in thanksgiving and hope; trusting that somehow the ongoing visitation of angels will lead us to good fortune.

II

What about that second milestone by the brook called Jabbok, that all night struggle so filled with perplexity and peril? The story stirs up all kinds of questions. With whom is Jacob wrestling? Man or God? Esau or himself? Adversary or advocate? What does it mean that Jacob receives a wound? That he is given a new name? What does this milestone moment mean for you and me? Tough questions, as we like to say.

With whom is Jacob wrestling? Certainly Esau is a good candidate. Jacob knows that tomorrow he must face the brother he cheated long ago, the brother who may well still carry the murderous rage from which Jacob fled for his life. Like all of us Jacob wrestles with the possible consequences of his past betrayals. Like all of us Jacob wonders whether the one he has hurt will hate him or forgive him. Is there anyone here who has never wrestled at midnight with just such questions? Jacob is surely wrestling with the brother he must face in the morning.

But just as surely Jacob is wrestling with himself. Surely he is asking himself the question that all of us eventually must ask: "What sort of person have I become? Have I, in years of accommodation to convenience, ambition, convention, given away some essential part of myself? Has a lifetime of maneuvering for advantage left permanent scars on my soul?" Whatever our fears about facing those we have hurt, I suspect that for all of us the person we most dread to confront – the person whom we cannot fool nor impress nor avoid – is the person in the mirror. Is there anyone here who has not had a few such midnight wrestling matches?

But is not Jacob also wrestling with God? In the morning he dusts himself off and says with awe: "I have looked on the face of God and lived!" Tradition speaks of Jacob's opponent as an angel – somewhere between human and divine. The ambiguity is perhaps intentional and inevitable. Someone has said, "We never get God alone, without all the complexities and unresolve of the neighborhood. And we never get the wronged brother alone, without the threatening face of God." When we wrestle with our sister or brother, or with our own deepest self, we also wrestle with the Spirit of God. And, as Jacob says the next day to his forgiving brother, "seeing your face is like seeing the face of God – since you have received me with such favor."

Is the one with whom Jacob wrestles an adversary or an advocate? Surely the answer must be both. When we face those we have wronged, when we face up to our own failures, when we face the loving God whom we have ignored or fled – we stand accused. Even if the one we face proves to be able and willing to forgive us.

The surprising discovery that Jacob will make is that his brother Esau is much more ready to forgive than Jacob, with his preparations and prayers and peace offerings, could have imagined. In the same way the amazing discovery all of us make, both with persons we have hurt and with the God we have feared, is that forgiveness is much more real and more likely than we had suspected, that those we had seen as adversaries often prove to be advocates. Perhaps we fear that others will not forgive because we find it so hard to forgive ourselves.

What does it mean that Jacob is wounded? There is no clear answer in the story itself. And yet a wound, a limp, a scar from the struggle seems to make sense, doesn't it? Struggles usually leave us with wounds.

Perhaps the wound is simply the price Jacob pays for the choices he has made. Perhaps we can think about Jacob's limp as a kind of spiritual scar for his past misdeeds. Or perhaps the wound is simply to his ego. Don't we all feel wounded when we, like Jacob, have to face the fact that our solemn vows are sometimes self-serving, that our covenants are riddled with compromise, that our nicest face is often a mask for not-so-nice motives, that everything we do – or fail to do – has a price that only we may know?

To struggle with who we have become, what we have done or left undone, whom we have hurt or neglected – to face ourselves without evasion or excuse is a struggle from which we can only come away limping. Listen to these words of Aeschylus:

He who learns must suffer. And even in our sleep, pain that cannot forget falls drop by drop upon the heart. And in our despair, against our will, comes wisdom to us by the awful grace of God.

What does it mean that Jacob receives a new name? Certainly up to this point in his life the name of Jacob has described his character. The name "Jacob" means "supplanter," and every story thus far shows us a man always trying to get the advantage – with his brother, his father, his uncle, even with God.

In the struggle by the brook Jacob is given a new name along with his wound. He is to be called "Israel." The word means "He who struggles with God." In his midnight wrestling match Jacob no longer tries to survive by trickery, no longer bargains with man or God for the best deal. He strives, he pleads, he prays for a blessing. And the blessing is a new name, a new identity. Jacob receives the name "Israel," a name that will live in his children and their children. A name that lives to this day. Why is he blessed? Not because he has been a particularly good man, or even because he is about to become one. He is blessed because he has struggled to come to terms with his brother, his God, himself. At the deepest level, beneath the trickery and the ambition, Jacob, now Israel, is a man who doesn't give up the struggle. And for that he receives a blessing.

So what can we see in these milestone stories? What do they say to us that can enable us to face our own future with promise and our past with peace?

At Bethel, Jacob – and you and I – make the first important discovery: "surely the Lord is in this place and I didn't know it." That is the discovery that can set us on the road in hope and confidence, the discovery that indeed the gate of heaven is wherever we stand.

At Peniel, Jacob –and you and I – make the second important discovery: "I have looked upon the face of God and lived." That is the discovery that can enable us to face God and acknowledge who we have become, trusting that we will come away from such a meeting with a limp, perhaps; a blessing, for sure; and maybe even a new name.

REFUGEES

In the small Georgia city where I spent my adolescence the social level of one's family was measured, quite literally, by altitude. Augusta, built as an outpost a hundred miles up the Savannah River from the coast, burrowed its old downtown right into the levee, so that those who lived near the river were literally at water level most of the time. For many months of the year this meant high humidity and minimal breeze. In pre-air-conditioning days, it meant steamy days and oppressive nights. So those who could afford to do so bought or built houses on what was called simply, 'The Hill." It wasn't much of a hill by the standards of Appalachia or Colorado, but for Augustans seeking a breath of cool air, gaining a perch on the side or top of the Hill was a move toward all that was good and true and beautiful.

My family lived within three blocks of the levee. I could ride my bike along the top for miles, and I could walk downtown in the evening to watch the baseball scores being posted on the blackboard at the back of a slightly unsavory place called Home Folks Cigar Store. There were definitely advantages to living downtown. I was not dependent on my parents to drive me places, since my feet, my bike and the city bus took me almost anywhere I wanted to go. And I certainly was introduced to a wider slice of life (like Home Folks Cigar Store) than my Hill dwelling friends.

Just the same, those on the Hill seemed to breathe a different atmosphere socially as well as literally. Their parents were doctors and lawyers. Their homes were more substantial and better furnished than our row house apartment. They applied without debate to the small and expensive liberal arts colleges that seemed out of range to me. The friends I knew best were Episcopalians.

During these years I felt a lot like a refugee. I lived in one world, visited in a second, felt most at home in a third.

There were the boys in the neighborhood with whom I played ball in the next door playground and hung out on a neighbor's front steps in the warm evenings. George and Sonny and J.C. were aiming to finish high school and then settle into the kind of jobs that their fathers had. Sonny's father told my parents at our high school graduation that he was proud because his son had gone farther in school than anyone in the family before him.

Then there were the doctors' sons. Zack and Righton were the Episcopalians who lived on the Hill. Zack's family, in fact, lived at the very top of the Hill on a curving drive appropriately named Comfort Road. I knew them because we were in Latin class together, a bridge that gave me what access I had to their world. We took the bus across town to visit each other. Their parents were cordial to me, and my mother was pleased when Zack and Righton came to our house. As far as I can remember, our parents never met.

On a plateau between the downtown neighbor guys and the Hill dwelling doctors' sons were Mike and Billy, two upward looking flatlanders like me who lived in one world and longed for the other. Both Mike and Billy lived in houses even more modest than mine, somewhere in between downtown and the Hill. Both had aspirations to professional status far beyond their parents' achievement – Mike in medicine and Billy in dentistry. Billy and I rode the city bus to play golf at the public course. Mike brought me home from school whenever he had the family pickup.

My relationship with these three circles of friends

reflected clearly just what we shared and what we did not share.

I felt at ease with the boys of the neighborhood. We shared a place and a daily life. But I never felt fully at home with them, for they did not share my dream. I liked spending time with the doctors' sons, for we had similar dreams. But I could not feel at one with them in any complete sense, for we were only visitors in each other's worlds, and what they looked forward to as a given was for me a distant hope. I felt most at home with those who shared my journey – fellow refugees who were leaving the same Egypt, walking the same long road, looking for a new country. We spent our time together, fittingly enough, in motion rather than at rest.

As I suspected might be true, I never crossed paths with either Zack or Righton after we graduated from high school, although I have learned from newspaper and alumni accounts that both have died. My fellow refugees Mike and Billy both achieved their dreams of careers in medicine. I have no knowledge of Sonny, J. C. or George.

A STUDY IN TOLERANCE

The king ordered Joab . . . saying, "Deal gently for my sake with the young man Absalom."

II Samuel 18:5

The tragic story has its beginning eleven years earlier when David's son Amnon rapes his half sister Tamar. Tamar's brother Absalom murders Amnon to avenge his sister, then spends three years in exile from their father the king. He is eventually granted an official pardon by David, but father and son are never reconciled. David shuns Absalom, neither speaking to him nor allowing him into his presence. Over the years Absalom's bitterness and his ambition prompt him to take the lead in a rebellion against his father the king.

    When I was a little boy my Uncle Dave sang a song that I thought had been written especially for me. It began, "Little David, play on your harp. Hallelu! Hallelu!" I heard stories about little David the shepherd boy and his wonderful harp. When I had grown up a bit, I discovered that little David had too. He had in fact become larger than life, a heroic figure among many legendary biblical figures. Whether he was winning (as in Goliath) or sinning (as in Bathsheba) he did it big. When he gave words to his deepest feelings, they were eloquent words, whether he was repenting (*"create in me a clean heart, 0 God"*) or lamenting (*"how are the mighty fallen in the midst of battle"*). Even in the story of Absalom, a story of rebellion and betrayal, of death and mourning, David is a tragic figure, like something out of Shakespeare. And his words on hearing of his son's death are powerfully moving, *"O my son, Absalom! Would I had died instead of you, O Absalom, my son, my son!"*

It may seem hard to identify with this ancient warrior/poet/king in his epic adventures. Next to his story our own seems, well, ordinary. But let me suggest that this story may come closer than you would imagine. Think for a moment about the main characters:

Here is Absalom, a good looking, charming young man, exiled for acting violently to avenge his sister, hurt and angry at being rejected by his powerful father. Here is David, a troubled leader, struggling to resolve the conflict between keeping his kingdom intact and protecting his son. Here is Joab, a hard-nosed chief of staff, accustomed to doing the dirty work, playing the power game with little time for scruples. Stuff for Shakespeare, certainly. Maybe even for a movie. But how does it speak to us? How can we find ourselves in the story?

Well, if you've ever loved someone deeply – a son or daughter perhaps – and watched helplessly while he/she went down a destructive path, you might feel at home in David's story. If you've ever had someone you trust ignore your words and your interest to take matters into his own hands, you may know how David felt about Joab. If you've ever learned of the premature death of a dear one, especially if that death happened when the two of you were in a state of estrangement, then this story will feel familiar to you.

The most famous words of the story are, of course, David's words of lamentation. And there are in his words some lessons about genuine mourning. David expresses his grief without anger, without blame, without bitterness. So much of our grieving revolves around three refrains: "He was no good", "I'm no good", "life is no good". But David's grief is pure grief, pure sadness, purely vulnerable, helpless mourning.

But the words I want to focus on are a little less famous. They strike me as important for how we live our lives. Buried in this heroic story they may seem strikingly unheroic. You might even think at first glance that they are weak words. When he sends his generals out to put down the rebellion, David pleads with them, *"Deal gently for my sake with the young man Absalom."*

"Deal gently," says David. With an ambitious and violent and rebellious young man who has twice taken the law into his own hands? Hasn't David heard about getting tough on repeat offenders? Doesn't he know about "zero tolerance"? Apparently not. In fact I have come to think of this moment in David's career as a study in tolerance. And I believe that there is something important for us to learn about how tolerance is born.

First we must understand that tolerance is not the same thing as weakness or indifference, although sometimes we tolerate things for one or both of those reasons. But no one could accuse David of being a weak man. And all of us know that he could and did speak and act with passion. He was not tolerant because he was indifferent or weak. I can name four understandings that give birth to true tolerance such as we see in David.

First, tolerance is born when I understand that the needs and aspirations of others are as important to them as mine are to me. Perhaps David remembered his own ambition as a young man. Perhaps he had become aware of the frustration of his son at being treated as an outcast. Francis Bacon once said, "Why should I be angry at a man for loving himself better than me?" Why indeed should I expect everyone else to be as interested in my agenda as I am?

Second, tolerance is born when I understand that there are limits to my own perspective and experience and virtue.

Perhaps David recalled his own abuse of power with the soldier Uriah. Perhaps he understood that his unwillingness to take his son back had played a part in Absalom's rebellion. Reinhold Niebuhr wrote these words: *No virtuous act is quite as virtuous from the standpoint of our friend or foe as it is from our standpoint; therefore we must be saved by the final form of love which is forgiveness.* If I myself must finally hope for forgiveness, I do well to be a bit more tolerant of the failures of others.

Third, tolerance is born when I look deeply enough into the life of the one whom I see as enemy and realize that he too is suffering. Perhaps David remembered his suffering when he was exiled by Saul. Perhaps he understands a bit of his own son's suffering. Someone has written: *When you begin to see the suffering in the other person, compassion is born, and you no longer consider that person as your enemy . . . The moment you realize that your so-called enemy suffers and you want him to stop suffering, he ceases to be your enemy. . . Loving your enemy is only possible when you don't see him as your enemy anymore.*

Finally, tolerance is born when I understand that vengeance is a choice that destroys as much in me as it destroys in the object of my resentment. Perhaps David remembers how Saul's taste for revenge had a part in destroying him. Perhaps he has simply discovered from living that the desire for revenge might be strong but that the price is hardly worth it. Lewis Smedes talks about "giving up the right to get even." This is, he points out, the only way to put hurt behind us, since "we never bring closure to vengeance." The other person can never hurt enough to satisfy us. There is great wisdom in the word of scripture: "Vengeance is mine. I will repay, says the Lord." Tolerance means giving up the right to get even.

So, why spend so much time on such unheroic stuff as

tolerance? Because I believe that genuine tolerance requires a quiet kind of heroism that we underestimate. Genuine tolerance is hard to learn. It is hard because we cling to the sweet illusion that we are a bit more right than anyone else. It is hard because we shrink from the labor of searching out the needs and concerns of those who differ from us. It is hard because we are reluctant to give up what we imagine will be the lovely taste of payback. It is hard because we are afraid that others will look down upon us as weak or soft – that they will, in a word, be intolerant of our efforts at tolerance.

Why is it important? Today's word from Paul puts it very simply: *Put away all bitterness and wrath and anger and slander, together with all malice, and be kind to one another, tenderhearted, forgiving one another as God in Christ has forgiven you.* The invitation of Jesus makes it simpler still. We are all invited to his table – those whom we like and those who rub us the wrong way, those who treat us tenderly and those who treat us shabbily, those we tolerate and those who tolerate us. We, no less than they, are recipients of God's amazing grace. At God's table we are equals.

THE SECRET GARDEN

Many persons who grew up one or two generations back were introduced, by way of a parable, to the mystery and power of what we now call group therapy. The parable took the form of a children's story called *The Secret Garden* by Frances Burnett.

Three children discover an abandoned, overgrown garden behind a high stone wall and a locked gate, a garden closed by the owner of the English country manor after the death of his beautiful young wife. The owner has withdrawn into his work, abandoning to the care of housekeepers his fragile, lonely and crippled son. As companions to the unhappy young master come a girl embittered by the loss of her parents, and a boy of the nearby village, uneducated and impoverished, but gifted with a deep sense of connection to the world of nature.

The three children meet secretly to clean, tend and restore the garden. In the process they achieve much more. The self-pitying cripple learns to walk; the bitter, spoiled girl finds a reason to live; the village boy makes two valued friends.

How does this story of children in a garden tell a parable of the process and power of group therapy? It describes how three unlikely friends come together again and again in a secret place, each bringing hurts or deprivations as well as strengths and resources of which they may be only vaguely aware. It describes how they clean out the tangle of old, overgrown brambles and, in the process, help each other nurture new growth in place of the old. Several elements of the process seem essential for gardening or for therapy.

First, the garden meeting place is secret. Why does this matter? Because we, like those children, sometimes need a safe, private place to uncover old wounds, untangle old brambles, learn to take the first clumsy steps toward a new way of walking in the world. It is hard to discard our crutches when we fear we may fall on our faces, hard to take off our mask when we think our ugliness will repel those whose love we need, hard to expose our tears to what we sense are uncaring eyes. The privacy of the group offers a safe place to practice our humanity.

Second, the gardening is done in the company of several unlikely companions. Why? Because we may need privacy, but we do not need solitude for bur gardening. Companions help overcome our self-imposed isolation, our sense of specialness, our self-pity. They help us discover that we are more alike than different, that persons we would disdain to know have something to offer us and that people we fear can, if we will risk it, be trusted. The story of the secret garden is, like group therapy, a story of the healing power of friendship.

Third, gardening involves pruning, re-planting and weeding over an extended period of time. Gardening, like therapy, is not a get-fixed-quick pastime. Nor is it simply a comfortable, supportive gathering for a fast game of "Ain't it Awful." Just as the children in the garden challenge the crippled boy's defeatism and the girl's bitter self-pity, so companions in group therapy offer challenge as well as comfort, honest feedback as well as hope. There are habits of thought to be pruned, new self-concepts to be planted, new ways of speaking or acting to be nurtured. The damage done in years of neglect, abuse or crippling self-hate cannot be undone except by long hours of patient gardening.

Finally, gardening means learning to ally ourselves to the healing and life-giving forces of nature that are around and within us. In the story the village boy fills the role of therapist. He is not superhuman, not stronger or better than his companions. But he has acquired a perspective and a wisdom that he passes on to them, a wisdom about how things—and people— grow. Being more in touch with his own natural self and less encumbered with the false selves and unhealthy attitudes of his companions, he is able to help them discover their own kinship to nature, so that gradually they learn to feel at home in a world in which they had thought themselves to be aliens.

The healing power of the group lies in all of the relationships between its members. The therapist is only a more experienced gardener who knows something about how to prune and how to plant. Therapy works the way gardening works, through patient cultivation of the natural gifts that God has given us.

HOW WE RESPOND TO THE CHILD

Rise, take the child and his mother and flee to Egypt, and remain there until I tell you, for Herod is about to search for the child, to destroy him.

Matthew 2:13

The story brings us back to reality with a crash. Hard upon all the beautiful Christmas words and images comes a brutal reminder of the dangerous world into which Jesus was born and of the difficult journey that began for him and his family. The focus in this story is not so much on the Christchild as it is on two persons and how they respond to him; how one threatens him and one protects him.

It sounds like a typical story of bad guy/good guy. We identify with the good Joseph and admire him for protecting the precious new messiah; we are appalled at the wicked Herod and all the bad guys who attack Christ. It is tempting to read this story as a "we/they" story, but it is not honest. For as much as we would like to think of ourselves as Josephs, there are times when we would rather send the Christ into exile, times when we are more like Herod, even when we are proudly claiming our role as defenders of the faith.

Today I invite you to do something hard. I invite you to think of this story as a story about yourself – about *both sides* of yourself.

The fact is that sometimes we are like Herod. We feel a need to protect our interests, even if it means getting rid of anyone whose presence threatens our comfort and our security. Of course our weapons are not Herod's weapons.

We have neither the stomach nor the power for massacres (although sometimes when we act collectively a lot of innocents do get slaughtered). But our targets are not just terrorists who threaten our physical safety.

The fact is that there are many people who threaten our security, and a lot of them are children. There are children who threaten our peace of mind by being homeless when we are warm and secure; children who offend our contentment by being poor when we are well off; children who are sick and untreated when we have pretty good insurance.

And then there are those modern counterparts of Joseph and Mary and Jesus whom we call refugees, whose eyes of misery accuse us on the Evening News. In our own land there are the various untouchables, victims of AIDS or addiction or abuse whose very existence challenges our comfortable notion that things are pretty much the way they need to be.

There is a Herod in you and me that wishes into exile – or at least into invisibility – those children of God who disturb our peace. There is a Herod in us that clings to our status quo power by shutting out the voice of the powerless. Our weapons are not usually Herod's weapons. We do not slaughter these innocents. We just turn off the TV or turn our minds to more pleasant things. The Herod in you and me exiles those who disturb us by wiping them from our consciousness, and even, sometimes, from our conscience. Our choice of weapons is indifference.

But sometimes we are like Joseph. Sometimes we reach out to our fragile brothers and sisters and embrace them. Sometimes we allow ourselves to be touched by the needs of the world's children and to care for them. At our best there is in each of us a nurturing mother or protective father that is able to see beyond our own children and give something of ourselves to others.

It is the Joseph in you that brings extra food for a family not your own, that keeps prodding our wealthy nation to provide some measure of medical care for those who cannot afford it. It is the Joseph or Mary in you that spends time and energy building homes for people whom you have never met, people who have no claim on you except the fact that they share living space on this small planet. It is the Joseph in you that is guided by a dream that tells you to open your shut-up heart to those who need what you have to give.

I think we all know the Joseph within us. And, if we are honest, we also know the Herod. And we know that there is a constant struggle within us between generosity and greed, compassion and indifference, love for all of God's children and disdain for those children whose presence disturbs us. Joseph and Herod struggle within us. Which one wins each day, or even each moment, depends on how we respond to the third character in this disturbing, yet hopeful, little story.

How do Herod and Joseph respond to the child? One sees him as a threat, a disturber of his peace. The other sees him as a gift, a bringer of something new. Herod, and the Herod in me, sees the refugee on TV or the sick child on welfare and wants to get rid of these disturbers of our peace by moving on to a more pleasant channel. Joseph, and the Joseph in you, sees the child in the manger – or the ghetto – as God's gift of new life, a brother or sister who may bring some new gift to the world or at the very least will draw us beyond ourselves and stretch our capacity to care.

So the question is, how do we see the child – as a disturber of the peace or as a bringer of a gift? The answer, of course, is both. The child is a disturber of your peace whenever your peace depends on keeping power and prosperity at the expense of ignoring your brothers and sisters. The child is a disturber of my peace whenever my

peace is built upon the lies I tell myself to justify my self-absorption.
But the child is also a bringer of a gift. Antoine de Saint Exupery, who gave the world the story of the Little Prince, wrote this account of what happened to him on a French train. I think that I hear the voice of Joseph.

The third class carriages were crowded with hundreds of Polish workmen sent home from France . . . In the dim glow cast by the night lamps into these barren and comfortless compartments I saw a confused mass of people churned about by the swaying of the train. . . . Looking at them I said to myself that they had lost half their human quality. These people had been knocked about from one end of Europe to the other by the economic current.

. . . A baby lay at the breast of a mother so weary that she seemed asleep. Life was being transmitted in the shabbiness and disorder of this journey. I looked at the father . . . the man looked like a lump of clay, like one of those sluggish derelicts that crumple into sleep in our public markets . . . between the man and the woman a child had hollowed himself out a place and fallen asleep. He turned in his slumber, and in the dim lamplight I saw his face. What an adorable face! A golden fruit had been born of these two peasants. Forth from this sluggish slum had sprung this miracle of delight and grace.

I bent over the smooth brow, over those mildly pouting lips, and I said to myself: This is a musician's face. This is the child Mozart. This is a life full of beautiful promise. Little princes in legends are not different from this. Protected, sheltered, cultivated, what could not this child become?

As we approach a new year I invite you to think on this story and the personal question it raises. How shall you, how shall I respond to the child whose face we see in this new Year of our Lord? Shall we allow the child to be both a disturber of our peace and a bringer of a gift?

Can you allow her to disturb your peace by opening your eyes to the needs of the least of your brothers and sisters, opening your hearts to their pain? Not just in the twelve days of Christmas but in the other eleven months of the year; not just in Bethlehem but in all the Egypts and Nazareths and refugee camps and trailer parks and third class coaches in which they live? And can you allow him to bring you a new gift by restoring in you a sense of community with these who have the same Father and Mother as we, by reminding you that each of these least ones may be in fact not your enemy but another little Mozart, another little Christ?

If we can do this, then we can be ruled more and more by our Joseph compassion and less and less by our Herod fears. Ask yourself each day, what child is this?

A DIFFERENT DRUMMER

Didn't you know that I must be about my Father's business?

Luke 2:49

Even though it is a familiar story, the gospel reading for today seems out of place. Only a week after the birth stories and songs of Christmas we find ourselves hearing about Jesus as a twelve year old who worries his parents. It may seem a little difficult to fast forward so abruptly, even for those of us who are accustomed to watching a life story in a two hour movie. But coming as it does on the eve of the New Year the story still has some telling questions to raise. So put on your space helmets and move with me from the stable to the city, from the babe in the manger to the adolescent in the temple.

What we have heard is the only incident in the canonical gospels that gives any glimpse at all into the life of Jesus between infancy and the public ministry he began at the age of thirty. The almost total silence of these "hidden years" has given scholars many opportunities to speculate. What was he doing? From whom did he learn? Did he travel as a young man – and if so, where? How did he come to the consciousness of mission that we see in full blossom at thirty?

The story of Jesus in the temple only hints at answers to these questions. And even those answers depend a lot on the bias of those who are asking them. Some Christians view this story as the story of a prodigy, rather like Mozart playing before the crowned heads of Europe at the age of three. I grew up with that image of Jesus, as a kid who knew all the answers from the beginning. Maybe you did too. It bothered me some, I must admit. I wondered why Jesus would have to bother to go to school if he knew everything. It bothered me more later on when I learned that such a view of Jesus has a theological name. It is called Docetism. It is considered a heresy. Docetism is so intent on affirming Jesus' special relationship to God that it makes him a kind of superboy, not really human at all. Which means that he is not really like you and me.

Another way of looking at the story is to view it as an early validation of this special relationship to God. Jesus is, so to speak, putting Mary and Joseph (especially Joseph) in their place. Joseph, after all, is only a kind of stepfather. One might, in this view, think of Jesus' words as simply the voice of a precocious messiah-in-waiting, a little impatient with his slow witted parents. A more recent variation on this view sees this story as an early reminder by Luke that the Jesus of whom he writes is one who challenges that venerable institution, the patriarchal family. Maybe so. The adult Jesus of the gospels certainly does not hold patriarchal traditions in high esteem.

Then there are those who remind us that the story as Luke tells it has strong echoes of the story, familiar to all his readers, of the call of Samuel. Jesus, Luke may be saying, comes from the line of those who were shaped and called to a special prophetic role.

Of course we can only guess at why Luke (and only Luke) includes this story in his gospel. We must not make too much of it or try to build a theology around it. But the story does suggest a couple of things that we may take to heart. To put it in a single sentence: Jesus is discovering, as all of us must eventually discover, that his true identity will be found only as he moves beyond those temporary identities that keep us all safe along the way. Or, to say it more simply:

Jesus is one who marches to the tune of a different drummer.

Listen again to the familiar words of Thoreau: *If a man does not keep pace with his companions, perhaps it is because he hears a different drummer. Let him step to the music which he hears, however measured or far away.* Certainly Jesus stepped to a different drummer. In this story it is different from that of his family; as an adult, it is different from his culture and even his traditional religion.

His drummer was different from his family. Like most adolescents he gave his parents some sleepless nights while he paid attention to that distant music. For parents, including Mary and Joseph, anxiety about growing sons and daughters is inevitable, because all good parents are trying to walk that narrow line between protecting their children and respecting them.

Sometimes we want to protect our children from the pain that we see coming their way, if they seem to be straying too far from what our experience tells us are the tried and true pathways. And – let's be honest – we also want to protect ourselves: sometimes from the pain of seeing them hurt, sometimes from the threat of having our own world upset if our adventurous or rebellious offspring challenge our guidance, our values, our judgment. What if they don't get away with it? What if they *do* get away with it?

But just as we want to protect our children, we also want to respect them as human beings with the right to choose their own way, even if that way seems to us to be fraught with danger and disappointment. Mary and Joseph, and all parents, must somehow learn not only to protect but to respect their growing son or daughter, not because Jesus was one of a kind, but because each of us is one of a kind.

We can also take note that Jesus had to strike a

balance. After telling us how Jesus somewhat rudely brushed off his mother's reprimand, Luke closes the vignette by saying that the young man was an obedient son as he continued to grow in every way. Like other growing sons and daughters, Jesus had to find a way to strike a balance between respect for his parents (who, after all, are trying to care for him in the best way they know) and respect for himself in his search for the path on which the drummer is leading him.

As an adult, Jesus' drummer was different from that of his culture or his religious tradition. We get a hint of that even in this story, hearing how the wise men in the temple were amazed at his questions and his answers. I don't think that their amazement is simply that of ordinary mortals in the presence of a prodigy. I suspect that their amazement had a touch of discomfort in it, discomfort that this peasant boy would ask such challenging questions or counter their conventional wisdom with what scholars have called his own brand of "subversive wisdom".

Over and over again the gospels tell how Jesus offered a deeper vision of the kingdom of God than people were hearing from their teachers. He spoke as a good Jew, but he called upon people to grasp a more authentic, more profound understanding of their own tradition. He challenged the patriarchy; he challenged the civil and religious authorities; he challenged their narrowness of vision, their accommodation to what have been called the "domination systems" of their day. "You have heard," Jesus would say "but I say unto you." Jesus listened, and marched, to a different drummer.

We have said that he was discovering his identity – almost a cliché when speaking of adolescents. Perhaps it is a cliché because it is so profoundly true, not only for adolescents but for all of us.

Listen to what Thomas Merton has to say about

identity:

Our vocation is not simply to be, but to work together with God in the creation of our own life, our own identity, our own destiny. . . This means to say that we should not passively exist, but actively participate in God's creative freedom in our own lives. . . To put it better, we are even called to share with God the work of creating the truth of our identity. . . To work out our own identity in God. . . is a labor that requires sacrifice and anguish, risk and many tears.

Thomas Merton has more to say about identity, much more. For the moment, let these words be enough to remind us that finding our true identity is a lifelong search. We are so easily caught up in false identities: who we think others want us to be; who we dream of being when we do not want to be ourselves; who we believe ourselves to be in the depths of our self-loathing or in the heights of our self-deception.

I'll not go on. You all know about those false identities. You have all been captive to them at times, as I have. And you know, as I do, that the struggle toward an authentic sense of self is a lifelong struggle. What I want to suggest today is that there is a connection between finding that true self and listening for that different drummer. When we listen for that drumbeat and follow it, we are no longer defined by the voices of culture or family or marketplace or nation, but by the voice of Spirit within us.

Listening for that drumbeat may, at times, make us look like rebels. Even Jesus looked like a rebel at twelve, when he was following that inner music. As an adult he sometimes rebelled against the false identities that others tried to force on him. "Rebel" is not a permanent identity, though some people like to portray themselves that way. Rebel is a defense, a posture, a drawing of the line. God does not call us simply to be rebels. God calls us to discover and live out our true identity, to listen for the inner drumbeat and march to it.

James Weldon Johnson was a poet, an African-American who gave us the wonderful collection of poetic sermons called *God's Trombones*. He also wrote the words to a moving song called *Lift Every Voice and Sing*, which has come to be known as the Negro National Anthem. He was a man who knew who he was. His poetry called upon others to discover who they were and to hold on to that knowledge. Listen to the words of a man who had heard his drummer loud and clear:

I will not allow one prejudiced person or one million or one hundred million to blight my life. I will not let prejudice or any of its attendant humiliations and injustices bear me down to spiritual defeat. My inner life is mine, and I shall defend and maintain its integrity against all the powers of hell.

"My inner life is mine"! That is an affirmation each of us can make and carry with us into every new day and new year and new challenge that life throws at our feet. That is what Jesus was telling his parents, and what we, listening to the best voice within, can say to every voice that tries to lead us away from the person God is calling us to become.

THE PRODIGAL, THE PHILOSOPHER AND THE PASTOR

Here is a familiar story about leaving home:

. . the younger son gathered all he had and traveled to a distant country, and there he squandered his property in dissolute living.

Another familiar story:

I went to the woods because I wished to live deliberately, to front only the essential facts of life, and see if I could not learn what it had to teach, and not, when I came to die, discover that I had not lived.

Both the prodigal and the philosopher left home to discover life – one to the city and one to the woods. Leaving home is something all of us do. It is a part of living, even when the path we take is full of potholes.

Listen again to the two stories:

When he came to himself he said . . . I will get up and go to my father and say to him, "Father, I have sinned against heaven and before you . . . treat me like one of your hired hands" So he set off and went to his father.

And the other story:

I left the woods for as good a reason as I went there.

Perhaps it seemed to me that I had several more lives to live, and could not spare any more time for that one.

Both the prodigal and the philosopher found their way home after a time in the city and the woods. Like all of us, they found that they needed to keep moving, to respond to whatever it is within us that makes us restless for home. A gifted young seminarian put it this way: *the story of our lives is the story of wandering, of rejecting home ... and of seeking it as deeply and as passionately as we can. . . Home is the roost for our souls, the place where our soul settles down.*

It seems to me that we spend our lives looking for a roost for our souls, a place to settle down. Our search may take many forms and many turns. We may, like Thoreau, make a deliberate trip, a pilgrimage of discovery in which we focus on the essentials and listen to the voice within us that can help us define who we are and to whom we belong. Or we may be moved by crisis – a job loss, a divorce, a serious illness, a failure, a death. And each crisis may be for us a time of testing that forces us to seek a place where we feel more "at home".

There is nothing sinful about the search, nothing unusual about the restlessness that sometimes causes us to move on even from what seems a comfortable place. Making a home is more than building a house, even though we may invest huge quantities of energy and money in our home place. Sometimes we come to feel that our roosting place does not do for a resting place. The roost becomes a routine, the routine becomes a rut, and we find ourselves wanting to take wing. Remember the song of a young man named Pippin? *Rivers belong where they can ramble; eagles belong where they can fly. I've got to be where my spirit can run free; gotta find my corner of the sky.* The only final roost for our souls is God, who created us with a longing for home, so that our hearts are restless until they rest in God. In the meantime, our spirits are searching, finding, leaving, searching again. Some searches end in disaster, some in spiritual growth.

Pastors are often invited to witness such journeys – as confessor, guide, supporter, reminder of divine forgiveness. They are, in a sense, the designated companion for many of us. But sometimes the search is complicated by blind spots, crippling wounds, persistent illusions about the home we are leaving or the home we seek. At such times pastoral counselors may be a helpful resource for both pilgrim and pastor. As someone has said, the therapist/counselor is simply a slightly more experienced mountain climber who can walk with you, pointing out hazards and new paths. All of us are on a lifelong search for home. The roost for our souls is something we each must find for ourselves. But we don't have to find it *by* ourselves.

A NATION OF STRANGERS

You shall also love the stranger, for you were strangers in the land of Egypt.

Deuteronomy 10:19

Robert Benchley is reported to have made this observation: "The world is divided into two kinds of people; those who divide the world into two kinds of people and those who don't." It seems to me that most of the time the two kinds of people we name are "those who are like me" and "those who are not like me." My Kind of People and Everyone Else. Those whose ways are familiar to me and those whose ways are strange.

In some languages the word for *stranger* (or alien as it is sometimes translated) is the same as the word for *enemy*. We have two different words in English, of course, but I think that the emotional meaning is often the same. A stranger is someone I don't know, someone who seems different from me. An enemy is one whose differentness is in some way a threat to me

In Mark's story of the Syrophoenician woman (Mark 7:24ff), Jesus' disciples obviously saw the stranger as different enough to be something of a threat. She was a Canaanite, a member of a clan with a history of enmity for the Jews. A rough parallel today would, I think, be a visit by a Palestinian to a gathering of Jews. And Jesus, at first glance, seems to buy into their cultural bias (which was certainly also his cultural bias). The disciples want him to send her away, and indeed Jesus treats her very rudely at first. It is not until she challenges his prejudice that he discovers some common ground between this stranger and himself. We'll return to that part later.

But first, we need to ask ourselves why we have such a hard time with strangers? Why is it that we tend to equate alien with enemy? And what needs to happen within us – as it happened within Jesus – to overcome our fear of the stranger?

I

Is there a way in which we need to define people as strangers? I think so. There seems to be a way, or two ways, in which we need people whom we can call alien, or even enemy.

First, the Alien is our screen for projecting onto others the dark side of ourselves. We tend to blame others for things that we don't like to face in ourselves ("she doesn't like me" is easier to say than "I don't understand her"). And if the person or group is very different and their ways inaccessible to us, we do it all the more. Anne Fadiman has written a fascinating study of the conflict between well-meaning American doctors and equally well-meaning parents of a Hmong child with epilepsy. The title of the book is taken from the Hmong word for epilepsy: *The Spirit Catches You and You Fall Down*. Listen to her speak of this alien group.

It could not be denied that the Hmong were genuinely mysterious—far more so, for instance, than the Vietnamese and Cambodians who were streaming into the United States at the same time (the early 1980's). Hardly anyone knew how to pronounce the word "Hmong". Hardly anyone . . . knew what role the Hmong had played during the war, or even what war it had been, since our government had succeeded all too well in keeping the Quiet War quiet. Hardly anyone knew they had a rich social history, a complex culture, an efficient social system, and enviable family values. They were therefore an ideal blank surface on which to project xenophobic fantasies.

Xenophobic fantasies! What a wonderful way to describe the fearful imaginings that we create about those whose looks or ways are foreign to us. All of us know something about projection. Family therapists are so used to it that they have a special term that they use when a family comes in for counseling. One person in the family is called the "identified patient". That is, this is the person that the rest of the family chooses to designate as "the problem".

Nations do the same thing. It is convenient to call a particular nation an "evil nation" or a "rogue nation" so that the rest of the family of nations can keep their own self-image clean. It is easier to say that other nations are just envious and bitter toward the U.S. than to look at how we may provoke that bitterness with our careless and conspicuous consumption. It is easy to focus on the strangeness of other cultures, as though our own culture (our kind of people) were somehow the standard for the rest of the world. Having people called strangers gives us someone to blame when things don't go well between us and our neighbors.

Second, the Alien enables us to draw together into something bigger than ourselves. Eric Hoffer, writing about what he calls the *True Believer*, comments that "a mass movement can exist without a god, but not without a devil." It seems that we need an enemy, not only to blame for things we don't want to face in ourselves but to help unite us with others who are more or less like us. We want to belong to a movement, a group, a cause. We are tempted by ads for a corps that needs "just a few good men." We are moved when Henry V rallies his men the night before Agincourt, calling them "we few, we happy few, we band of brothers."

Jesus' disciples liked to think of themselves as God's people as opposed to "those other people". Some have suggested that many Americans had a hard time when the Cold War ended. It seemed that we could not define ourselves without having someone to be against. Now, in the terrorists we have a real enemy again. The problem now is that our enemy has no face, so the temptation is to call anyone we fear or dislike a "terrorist" or even a "potential terrorist." As someone has said, "When you're bitten by a snake, every rope looks dangerous." But calling every rope a snake is like calling every stranger an enemy. Some have learned the hard way, and many never learn, that paranoia can become a self-fulfilling prophecy.

II

Well, what can release us from our fear of the stranger and from our deeply rooted habit of dividing the world into two kinds of people? What was Jesus able to call up in himself that enabled him to overcome his own cultural bias and reach out to an alien woman?

Jesus, after his first negative reaction, was able to see beneath the alien surface a woman who loved her child, loved her enough to suffer humiliation on the chance that she might find healing for her child. He was able, after first dismissing her as one of the dogs, to recognize in her a faith in the goodness of God that transcended any surface differences. Beneath her alien ways he was able to see a depth of human faith and love very much like his own. How could he do this? Perhaps because he was mature enough in the spirit to realize that surface differences are not important. Perhaps because he remembered the word that we heard this morning, a word that is deeply rooted in Jewish tradition: *"Do not turn away the stranger. You know the heart of the stranger, for you were strangers in the land of Egypt..."*

"You know the heart of the stranger." Jesus did. He certainly must have felt like a stranger many times, not only among Romans and Canaanites but even with his fellow Jews. And you and I know the heart of the stranger too, don't we? Haven't you had moments of feeling like a stranger – maybe in a group of people who know each other better than they know you? Or even with those to whom you are known, when your thoughts and feelings seem to set you apart. Even as loveable and convivial a man as the poet Robert Burns had times that caused him to write these lines:

*"I've seen sae mony changefu' years,
On earth I am a stranger grown;
I wander in the ways of men,
Alike unknowing and unknown."*

"Do not turn away the stranger," says the Lord, "for you were strangers in the land of Egypt."

III

It can still happen, even in our fearful, conflicted world. On the first day of the new millennium, our daughter Kate was married to a young man named Hesham, who had come to America from Egypt some four years before. A year or two later Hesham took Kate to Cairo to meet his family. She was, during that visit, a stranger in the land of Egypt. Hesham and his family were able to make her welcome. I like to think that Hesham was able to welcome the stranger in the land of Egypt because he himself had been an Egyptian stranger in the land of Carolina. And I like to think that Kate was able to reach out to that

Egyptian stranger because she had learned in her own life how to see the deeper places in human beings beneath whatever surface strangeness might seem to separate them.

It can still happen, even among nations. America has been called a "nation of strangers", a land inhabited by aliens who found a way to live together. Every Fourth of July it is worth celebrating that America found its strength in this very fact; that where everyone was a stranger no one was a stranger. Each new family was able, in time, to give up the old name by which they had been called – Italian, Russian, Irish, Greek, Polish. All, in time, took on a new name – American.

Today we live in a world of strangers, aliens who sometimes look like enemies. We are no longer insulated from one another by oceans. The time has come for us to find a way to transcend the differences that threaten to destroy us. The time is far past for us to turn away from the path of self-destruction that we and other nations are walking – whether self-destructive violence or self-destructive blindness. We need to realize a common ground more basic than American or Egyptian, Israeli or Palestinian, black or white, gay or straight, Christian or Muslim, European or Arab.

Listen to these simple words from a man who does not describe himself by any nationality. His name is Terence. Let his words speak for him:

I am a human being; therefore I consider nothing human alien to me.

Can we say that? Can we reach beneath our fear, our prejudices, our cultural and religious parochialism, our addiction to dividing the world into two kinds of people? Can we finally know that beneath all our differences we are human beings every one, and that nothing human is alien to us? Can we remember that we are all children of the one Creator who gives us life, loves us, nurtures us, and calls us to love one another?

God help us to welcome the stranger so that we may discover in the stranger a sister or a brother.

THE FACE ACROSS THE TABLE

When I first heard of the shooting I felt the same shock as many others in the community. My wife and I had been friends of the family for many years. We knew Martha* as a lively, funny, outspoken redhead who gave good parties, catered weddings, and made herself felt in her little rural community in a variety of ways. Her husband Richard was a quiet man, a little aloof behind his dark beard. Martha seemed to do the talking for both of them.

Fragments of the story filtered through phone conversations, then were confirmed on the local radio. Martha was dead, shot in her own home by her seventeen year old son. Richard, wounded by a second shot, had been helicoptered to the hospital. Jeremy, the tall red-haired boy who so mirrored his mother's looks and breezy style, was in detention in the county jail, charged with murder.

I was asked to lead a memorial service. Twenty year old Rachel, the only surviving family member not in hospital or jail, put the service together with the help of Martha's sister Peg and a few close friends. As I led the large crowd of stunned neighbors and relatives through a time of reflection and prayer, I confessed that I was acutely aware that this family, stricken down by tragedy, was not so different from all other families. Many who spoke to me that day and on following days confirmed that awareness. Many were shaken by the violence that lay so close to the surface in this family that reminded them so much of their own.

On the afternoon of the memorial service I visited Jeremy at the Adult Detention Center. It was the first of many visits. In the beginning we met only in one of the visitors' booths, with a glass window between us and telephones on either side to carry our voices through the wall. For most of the early visits Jeremy cried. I listened and tried to touch him through the glass.

Eventually I became a regular visitor, listening to Jeremy's anxieties about his coming trial, his fears about the future, his sadness at the shattering of the family, his confused, fragmentary recollections of that awful January day. When I learned how to request it, we were allowed to meet in the tiny library, which was stocked with donated paperbacks of all hues. We no longer had to use telephones to carry our voices through the glass wall. We could, from time to time, even touch.

Those who knew of my interest in Jeremy continued to ask about him. Their questions, like my own, reflected a puzzled, disturbing search. Everyone seemed to be groping for something to explain an event that had about it a kind of primal horror. What kind of kid could kill his mother? What kind of mothering could provoke such rage? What kind of family life could foster such tragedy? At the same time I heard a touching, sometimes tender concern for Jeremy, a concern that seemed to be moved by something deeper than compassion, though that compassion was real enough. It seemed to me that some who spoke their concern were voicing a sense of identity with the young man, although no one said it clearly.

And why was I drawn to him? Why was it that from the very beginning I knew what he would say when he finally talked of the feelings toward his mother that erupted with such destructive fury? I remembered that from the first word of Martha's death I had felt deeply for Jeremy, even as I was shocked and saddened at the death of a woman I liked and admired. I recalled that when I first spoke to him through the glass I told him that I had not come to judge him but to be his friend. The questions persisted until the answer began to come clear in a conversation I had with Jeremy and with myself.

Whose face is looking back at me across the table? We sit in the small book-piled reading room of what is called the Adult Detention Center. He wears the bright orange of an inmate. Is he really one of those the cynical deputy calls the "young guns," a cluster of under-twenty first offenders held for varying degrees of violence?

Does the face that watches me belong simply to the kid next door, the friendly talkative son of my friendly talkative neighbor and her much less talkative husband? Or can there be someone else looking back at me, someone I have known for a long time?

"Some of the guys here say you can tell a murderer by looking at his face," he says. "But I tell them they're crazy. We don't look any different from anyone else." Under the protest I hear a question. Behind the troubled scowl I see him watching and waiting.

"I don't see a murderer when I look at you, Jeremy," I hear myself saying. "I see someone a lot like myself, except for one moment's loss of control." Is this then the face that looks back at me? Am I, in fact, looking into the face that greets me every morning in the mirror?

For both of us the question is a crucial one. He wants to know how to think of himself, whether he must, in fact, surrender to the deputy's label. He wants to know whether I see in him a different sort of human being, branded forever by some Cain-like mark. The answer I find and speak to him is clear. "You are not a label. You are a young man who has killed, and now you are living through the anguished aftermath of a moment of rage that changed forever your life and the life of your family. You have much pain to endure. But you are still a human being, not a label, a human being very much like me. We are, and will always be, brothers."

The question for me is also crucial. Am I really different from this young man? Or is there within me the capacity for destruction that overwhelmed him that awful afternoon? The answer again is clear. The only difference between me and my young brother is the difference of control in the presence of great stress. If I judge him with a label, whether "young gun" or "murderer," I judge myself, for I have murdered with my mind many times, just as that deputy has. The face across the table is mine.

My search becomes clearer as I discover and ponder the ancient words of the Roman poet Terence: humano sum; humani nil a me alienum puto. *I am a man. I count nothing human foreign to me...* Perhaps that is what lies behind the tenderness of those who inquire for the young man Jeremy. Perhaps they, like me, are inquiring for the soulmate whom they perceive beneath his orange clothes and deep crimson crime.

Words still more ancient catch my eye, words to wandering Jews who have left Egypt and struggle through wilderness: "You shall not oppress a stranger; you know the heart of a stranger, for you were strangers in the land of Egypt." Yes. I do know the heart of this stranger. And I know that he is no stranger. I do not know exactly what happened on that January day or the days that preceded it. I do not know why he lost control of his rage with such devastating results. But I know now that he is no stranger to me. Nor, I suspect, to those who ask with such secret urgency about his well-being.

In what way, then, have Jeremy and his family become vehicles for my own pilgrimage toward self-understanding? If I have, for Jeremy, been a messenger to help him recover his humanity, what has Jeremy been to me? The answer becomes clearer as I reflect on how my life has changed in the days and months since those shots were fired.

I have discovered my own kinship to all the players in the powerful human drama that was played out in Jeremy's home. I could be Martha, trying so desperately to bring about something good that I violate the one I hoped to save. I could be Richard, retreating in the name of peace and harmony from family conflict and leaving two people I love to struggle alone. I could be Jeremy, trapped against the wall of my own dependence on family, so that I can only turn in rage against those closest to me rather than find my way without them.

I have discovered a new compassion for each one who finds himself trapped, or believes himself to be trapped, in the web of loyalties, needs and affections called family.

I have become clearer about what I have to give to those around me, and what they have to give me. Not just good advice – that was Martha's mistake. Not support so distant that it feels like neglect – that was Richard's. When I chose, at the urging of a friend, to go to the jail, I did not know what I had to offer him. I dreaded that he would not speak and that I could not. I found myself – a reserved, even cautious, listener –speaking words of encouragement and hope more openly than I had imagined I could bring myself to offer. I found myself – a helper who seldom asked for help – sharing with colleagues my journey with Jeremy and asking for their prayers. I found within myself more than I had suspected. More capacity for caring, more willingness to ask for help, more courage to share my own pain.

I now know that what I have to offer Jeremy – and other Jeremys – is the same as what they have to offer me: a rediscovery of our common humanity. Nothing human is alien to me. Nothing in my own humanity is any longer alien. I find myself less a stranger to those who had seemed strangers. And to those close to me I am more able – and more willing – to share myself. Not my wisdom. Not my niceness. Just myself.

So it turns out that Jeremy's life-changing message to me is the one I had imagined was mine to him. The message is simple. Welcome the stranger –the Jeremy, the Martha, the Richard – within you. For you know the heart of the stranger.

* The names have been changed.

SAINTS PRESERVE US

Somewhere along the way I learned that Halloween means "hallowed evening." It is hallowed because it is the evening before All Saints. As a southern-bred Presbyterian I was never sure what to make of All Saints, since the only people I knew who talked about saints were my Episcopalian and Catholic friends. I pretty much filed away any serious thought about the meaning of sainthood until, at the funeral of my favorite uncle, I heard him referred to by the minister as a "Presbyterian Saint."

Well, so Presbyterians can have saints. And they can even be people we know! In case this seems to be a new idea to you, let me share with you something of how I have come to think about saints. What can saints mean to us? Or, to borrow a phrase, how can "saints preserve us"?

When we look at the meaning of "saint" over 2,000 years of Christian history we can see three ways that the word has been used. First, *saints are those persons in whom God seems to be visibly present.* In early Christian art the presence of God was represented by a kind of glow around the head called a "halo." We all know this meaning. A saint is a person whose life in some significant way is transparent to the presence of God. Each of us can think of a few people who fit that description. And we know that they have a powerful place in our lives. In the New Testament the word is used for everyone who belongs to God, so everyone is a saint. But in our common experience, it is – let's face it – a bit harder to see God in some than in others.

Second, *a saint is seen as a miracle worker.* In the

Roman Catholic tradition, no one is officially canonized – declared a saint – without some evidence that she or he can be credited with a miracle, usually more than one. These are usually miracles of healing, and they may happen either during or after the saint's lifetime. This is a more mysterious meaning of sainthood, implying that persons called saints are instruments of the power of God in some special way.

Third, *saints are seen as advocates for other people.* This, I have learned in my reading, is simply an extension of the fact that people pray for each other. A saint, then, is one who continues to pray for brothers and sisters in faith even after he or she has departed this life and gone into God's presence. A saint is one whose own life overflows with such love and goodness that he or she has a special influence with God. You could say that a saint is a sort of heavenly lobbyist on our behalf. Over the centuries a wonderful gallery of saints has been assembled to pray for us. St. Francis for animals and animal lovers; St. Elizabeth for pregnant women; St. Nicholas for children. We all know about St. Christopher, almost certainly mythical, the patron saint of travelers; and St. Thomas More, definitely not mythical, the Man for All Seasons and patron of lawyers. My newfound favorite is Christina the Astonishing, a Belgian saint who was known for one spectacular near death experience and was later sought out for wise counsel. She is the patron (or should we say matron?) for psychiatrists (and perhaps, I might add, pastoral counselors). Even nations have patron saints: St. Patrick for the Irish, St. Andrew for the Scots, St. David for the Welsh. (I have thought that if America had a patron saint we might be asking that saint to intercede for us a little extra right now).

Well, in our Protestant tradition we do not usually think of saints as miracle workers or as heavenly advocates (although it may well be that we are missing something). But I have come to think that there is still a way in which those whom we call saints have an important place in our faith journey. There is a way in which the saints do "preserve us."

They preserve our faith. When I was growing up I had many times of doubt about what was most real or most important in life. I had serious questions about God. But I also had my own experience with certain persons who, without knowing it, preserved my faith. My Aunt Lib struggled all of her life with depression, with illness, and with a difficult marriage. The constancy of her courage and good spirit were for me a model of faithfulness. She was my own Saint Elizabeth. My Uncle Dave, whom the minister called a "Presbyterian Saint," spent his long life opening his heart and his home to an amazing number of children, many of them strangers to him. His life was for me a model of generosity. He was my own Saint David.

Because these persons and others believed deeply and cared generously, because it was clear to me that God was visible in their lives, my own faith was preserved. In a real sense I borrowed from their faith when my own was shaky. I drew on their "spiritual capital," if you will. You might even call them miracle workers, for they worked in me a miracle of faith.

They preserve our vision. When I am tempted to grow cynical about human beings, I remind myself of those whom I think of as saints. When I feel discouraged by the power of evil in the world, whether the destructive, violent evil of terrorists or the passively self-centered evil of those who look the other way in the face of human suffering, it helps me to remember the saints I have known and still know. These saints preserve my vision of what human beings may become.

In a class once we struggled with the business of

forgiveness. "How," asked one person in the class, "can you forgive someone when justice has not been done, when innocent people are burdened for a long time because of that failure of justice?" No one had a quick answer. And then someone remembered a man who spent eleven years in prison for a crime he did not commit and was still able to forgive the woman who had mistakenly accused him. Another person reminded us of Nelson Mandela, who served twenty-eight years in prison and was still able to lead his country in establishing what was called a "Truth and Reconciliation Commission." These are surely saints, bearers of God's presence, preservers of a vision for humanity.

So, who are the saints who preserve you? Just the ordinary women and men who have touched your life, in whom God is visibly present, who awaken and preserve in you the miracle of faith or renew and enlarge for you a vision of the best that human beings can become.

One more word. Your saints need not be "saintly" in the usual sense of the word. Someone you remember may be a model of courage, another of good humor in times of difficulty. You may think of a feisty saint who taught you how to fight the good fight; a joyful saint who showed you how to laugh; even a prickly saint who taught you how to appreciate prickly people. It takes all kinds to make a heaven. It takes all kinds of saints to preserve our faith and enlarge our vision.

MY PLACE OR YOURS

The invitation seemed like a good opportunity to build good community relations. The Mt. Olivet Baptist Church, one of the African-American churches in our rural Virginia county, was celebrating the Thirty Fifth anniversary of its pastor. Joe Hackett had been pastor there slightly longer than I had been alive. He had welcomed me when I came to town to organize a new Presbyterian congregation. The invitation had gone, I am sure, to all the clergy of the area. I decided that I would go. My wife stayed home with our two toddlers.

It was a hot Sunday afternoon. The church was packed with church members, visiting clergy and old friends. By the time the service began I realized that I was a single small marshmallow floating in a large, warm cup of chocolate. No other white clergy had showed up. No other white faces were to be seen in the building.

The service was full of music and memories, tributes and testimonials. Every visiting clergyman was invited to bring greetings. I spoke as best I could for all of my absent colleagues; my words were greeted with warm applause. After a two hour service I was making my way out when the pastor said that I would, of course, join them downstairs for dinner. Of course I did, after a hasty phone call home to let Lynn know of my extended engagement.

I was seated at the long head table with Joe, his family and all the other clergy. Across the table from me were the Hacketts. Sitting next to Joe was his attractive daughter, flanked by her husband, a nice looking young man who seemed to be sweating as profusely as I. As we chatted I learned that he worked in a government office in Washington, that he and Joe's daughter had been married about as long as I. The young husband looked around the table at the assembled clergy and whispered to me, "Boy, I sure do feel out of place here!"

I am sure that the young man was speaking from the heart. I am equally sure that he had no idea how his feelings were a mirror of my own. I realized that my marshmallow discomfort was no greater than his unease at being, as he saw it, a lone sinner in a sea of ecclesiastical saints.

GOD'S BUCKET

This sermon has one point, surrounded by two poems. I asked if I could preach today because May 4 is special for Lynn and me. Forty years ago today we made our wedding vows, so I wanted the privilege of preaching what you might call a retrospective wedding sermon.

Those of you who know me a bit will not be surprised at the identity of the first poet. You may even guess the poem. From the gospel according to Shakespeare, Sonnet Number 116.

> *Let me not to the marriage of true minds*
> *Admit impediments. Love is not love*
> *Which alters when it alteration finds,*
> *Or bends with the remover to remove.*
> *Oh no! It is an ever-fixed mark*
> *That looks on tempests and is never shaken.*
> *It is the star to every wandering bark,*
> *Whose worth's unknown, although his height be taken.*
> *Love's not Time's fool, though rosy lips and cheeks*
> *Within his bending sickle's compass come.*
> *Love alters not with his brief hours and weeks,*
> *But bears it out even to the edge of doom.*
> *If this be error and upon me proved,*
> *I never writ, nor no man ever loved.*

The word of the Bard. Thanks be to Will for the right words about love; thanks be to Lynn for living them; thanks be to God for showing us what love is all about.

Of course this is a wonderful wedding poem, whether

you are reading it at the beginning of marriage as an expression of hope for what will be or after forty years of marriage in thanksgiving for what has been. The point of the poem, and of this sermon, is very simple: *people change; love does not*

I

One of the unsettling experiences of early marriage is the discovery that our partner is not quite the same person we thought we were marrying. Or, at least, he or she doesn't stay that way. Sometimes this discovery makes startled new spouses feel that they have been betrayed. But it is not necessarily that sinister.

They were not exactly lying to each other during that extended period of well meaning deception that we call courtship, although there was of course a certain amount of fooling (not to saying fooling around) during those months. They did try to "put their best foot forward," or at least to keep those two left feet out of sight. And in fact both co-operated in the benevolent business of interpreting in the most charitable way what might be questionable qualities in the other. Her little whims were "cute," his lower class tastes were simply "rough edges" that could, and would, certainly be smoothed off in time.

But apart from these early changes that had to do with deception (and self-deception) there were, the couple discovered, other changes. The partner got older, crankier, more forgetful, more eccentric. He didn't think her loveable whims were cute anymore. She was not as patient when his rough edges did not seem to get any smoother. What is worse, some things she used to enjoy doing seemed less enjoyable; some things he thought were important didn't seem to matter.

One fact of long marriage is this: tastes change, bodies

change, priorities and moods change. Even affections come and go, and come and go again. Further, we change in response to the changes in our spouses, so that we find it hard to know which came first, his change or hers.

When I was a young husband, and even a middle aged family man, I was known far and wide as a person with a very long fuse. Patience was my middle name. Days could go by, even weeks, without my raising my voice in anger, or even irritation. I was, in a word, wonderful. Well, I regret to report that I seem to be running short on long fuses. And I don't know where to go to get a fresh supply. To be completely candid, I have to say that Lynn is now more patient that I am.

Now, if it is unsettling to realize that our spouses have changed, it is alarming to face the fact that we have too. All kinds of questions begin to surface. What if she gets tired of the new me? What if he declares that he has been misled? What if my spouse wants to trade me in on a new model? Well, that is where the sonnet comes in. "Love," says Shakespeare, "is not love that alters when it alteration finds." Love doesn't change just because the beloved does. Affection, maybe. The length of one's fuse, certainly. But not love. If love changed when our partners did, there would be no long marriages, because change is one of the constant realities of married life.

To be honest, there are two other realities we must name. First, some marriages do not last. Sometimes the changes are so great that they overwhelm our best efforts. Sometimes the love with which we began is not as strong as we hoped and believed. Second reality. A long marriage is not always a sign of unalterable or undying love. Sometimes people stay together out of fear of change or convenience or even habit. Because of these realities it is always wise to be compassionate about marriages that fail and never wise to be smug about those that last.

Having said that, I still believe that the most important quality that holds a marriage together is the unaltering love of which Shakespeare speaks. And I can testify that my own marriage is evidence of that. I have been lucky in love beyond my best dreams and far beyond my deserving.

II

In marriage, people change; love does not. The same holds true for children. You might excuse newlyweds for being naïve about the reality of change, since they are blinded, or at least temporarily stunned, by that splendid insanity called infatuation. But you would think we would know better when it comes to children.

After all, children are supposed to change, even if spouses are not. People write books about how children change and when. They offer schedules and names to what are called "developmental stages." And of course we all know that there is one long and rather stressful developmental stage with the terrifying label "adolescence" (which has the unterrifying meaning of "becoming adult"). It is worth wondering, since becoming adult is supposed to be a good thing, why adolescence seems such a difficult thing.

Anyway, children change because that is what children are supposed to do. What makes it complicated, what calls for a lot of that unchanging love on the part of everyone, is that our children's changes do not always look the way we parents had in mind. They are not on the timetable we calculated. There are false starts, wrong turns, dead ends, rewinds, sudden fast forwards. And, of course, while our children are going through all these growing pains, we are changing too, so that *we* may not be in a good state of mind to cope with the unfolding drama in the room down the hall. Remember what I said about long fuses that get shorter?

Children change. So do parents. Love does not. Children need to know that their parents' love for them is unchanging. And parents can at least hope for some of the same.

III

Now, apart from the fact that I wanted to talk about marriage on my anniversary, why does this belong in a Sunday morning sermon? Because all I have said about unchanging love is based on the unchanging love of God that serves as the foundation, the model, the inspiration and the source of our loving.

Jesus said to his disciples, "which of you, if his child asked for bread would give him a stone? If you then, who are evil, know how to give good gifts to your children, how much more will your Father in heaven give good gifts to you!" Call this the "How Much More" principle. If we know how to love, it is because God has shown us how. We are created for love by love. As John puts it, "We love, because he first loved us."

This is where the second poem comes in, a poem by someone who is, I suspect, as unfamiliar as the first was familiar. It was written by a Persian poet named Hafiz a couple of centuries before Shakespeare. It is called "God's Bucket."

If this world was not held in God's Bucket
How could an ocean stand upside down
On its head and never lose a drop?
If your life was not contained in God's cup
How could you be so brave and laugh,
Dance in the face of death?
There is a private chamber in the soul that

*Knows a great secret of which no tongue can speak.
Your existence my dear, O love my dear,
Has been sealed and marked "too sacred,"
"Too sacred" by the Beloved - to ever end!
Indeed God has written a thousand promises
All over your heart that say,
Life, life, life is far too sacred to ever end.*

    I like to think of marriage and family as the cup God has made to hold us close in the intimate relationships we all need to become loving men and women.

    I like to think of the earth as the bowl God has shaped to hold the whole human family in a beautiful, nurturing natural world.

    I invite you to think of this vast, amazing and wondrous creation as God's Bucket, in which we are all held and embraced in the eternal, unchanging love of God.

    I believe that we can never fall out of God's Bucket. "Behold what love the Father has given us," says John, "that we should be called children of God. And indeed we are." Indeed we are.

ATTITUDE ADJUSTMENT

The hell to be endured hereafter, of which theology tells, is no worse than the hell we make for ourselves in this world by habitually fashioning our characters in the wrong way.
- William James

Earth might be fair and all men glad and wise.
Age after age their tragic empires rise,
Built while they dream, and in that dreaming weep:
Would man but wake from out his haunted sleep,
Earth might be fair and all men glad and wise.
- Clifford Bax

WHEN BEING WRONG IS ALL RIGHT

Jesus came to Galilee, proclaiming the good news of God and saying, "The time is fulfilled, and the kingdom of God has come near; repent, and believe the good news."
Mark 1:14-15

What kind of image comes to mind when you hear that someone is preaching about "repentance"? Perhaps you picture a man in a robe with a ragged beard, a Jonah-like cartoon character carrying a hand-lettered sign. If you have a taste for history, you may recall drawings of Jonathan Edwards, in his black robe and white tabs, thundering from his New England pulpit in an eloquent attempt to scare people out of hell – or vice versa. If you think in up-to-date images you may picture a sweaty televangelist, wrestling with his viewers for their souls and their contributions, so that his message comes across as: "Change your mind. And let me mind your change."

Repentance is not a very appealing word these days. It carries many connotations, most of them grim. We usually think it means something like, "Quit your meanness, give up all your favorite extracurricular habits, and feel bad about yourself three times a day."

But the word is really an honorable word, with a central place in biblical faith. It is literally the focal point of Jesus' first recorded preaching, as we read it in Mark, the earliest gospel: "The time has come, the rule of God is here and now, repent and believe the good news." In this context of good news, the word repent means more than "feel bad." It carries more a connotation of "change." Change your mind, change your heart, turn around and think again.

Now changing your mind is not something we like to do, especially when it means admitting we were wrong. We really don't like to admit we have been wrong. But let me remind you that there are times when being wrong is all right, when it can even be a relief to discover we are wrong.

Suppose you had lived your whole life with a mistaken idea about how to change a flat tire. And suppose you were stuck on a lonely road with the mistaken idea that the way to change your flat tire was to hold up the car with one hand while removing and replacing the tire with the other. And suppose, after a long, fruitless struggle, someone came along and introduced you to the good news about a wonderful source of power called "the jack." In order to take advantage of this good news, you would have to suffer the embarrassment of admitting that you had been operating with a wrong idea all your life. But it might be something of a relief. If someone shows us a better way, then, it may really be all right to be wrong.

Well, listen carefully. Because that is precisely what Jesus is trying to tell us. We think that we are supposed to be able to create security and well-being for ourselves and all of those we love. If only we have enough money, everyone will be okay. Wrong! Economic security can vanish with one board room decision at corporate headquarters, one accident, one chronic illness, one natural disaster. Hard work and virtue and insurance are no guarantee that you and your family will be safe and secure.

Another preacher said it centuries before Jesus: "Again I saw that under the sun the race is not to the swift, nor the battle to the strong, nor bread to the wise, nor riches to the intelligent, nor favor to men of skill; but time and chance happen to them all."

The fact is, we cannot control what may happen to us. That kind of power does not exist. In fact, power does not mean control – that is an illusion. Power means energy, the power that gives life and vitality, the power that is within each one of us as a gift of God. Not the power to control the world around us but the power to deal with what comes to us with courage and resilience and even humor. "Power," says the psalmist, "belongs to God." "The rule of God is here," says Jesus. "Change your mind and believe the good news. Open yourself to the source of all power."

Again, we think that we can, or should be able to, get people around us to do or be what we want them to do or be. We should be able to persuade or coerce or charm them into loving us, or respecting us, or at least accommodating us. We can do it, we persist in believing, if we are good enough, or smart enough, or persistent enough.

Wrong again! You can't make people love you. In fact, you can't make people do much of anything! Changing ourselves is hard enough. Changing other people is next to impossible. Oh, we can get a certain kind of compliance if we exert enough pressure. That is how laws work. But compliance is not change. Any ability we think we have to change other people is at best temporary and, at worst, an illusion. So "change your mind," says Jesus, "and believe the good news." The good news is that there is nothing you can do to earn love; the good news is that the love you need the most is already yours for the asking.

Why is it such good news to discover that we are so completely wrong? Because as long as we think that we must change that flat tire all by ourselves – without a jack – we are going to live with a lot of frustration. As long as you think that you can or should be able to provide perfect security by controlling the world around you, you will eventually feel angry or guilty or bitter or defeated. Because that kind of security is beyond us. And as long as I think that I can or should be able to get people to love me or accommodate me by fulfilling my dreams, I will probably be angry at them or at myself for what seems to be constant failure, because that kind of dream is one that cannot come true.

The sooner we change our minds and accept the truly good news that the real power that we need is already within us and the love that we seek has already been given us, the sooner we can quit straining after the impossible and blaming others or ourselves for our frustration.

If changing your mind is hard, there is one thing harder. That is changing your heart. In fact, I'm not sure we can do it alone. We can change our minds. It is not easy, and it is not quick. Learning to think in a new way about who we are and to whom we belong is a major task. It can take a lifetime. It means changing old habits of thinking and learning new ones. But it can be done.

But to change our hearts. Ah, that takes something or someone beyond us. I can teach myself to think differently, but I cannot make myself feel differently. Anyone who has ever tried to change a lifelong feeling of shame or low self-esteem knows that this is true. For our hearts to change they must be touched in a personal way. You will not feel loved until you have been touched by love. Your mind may be changed by the words of Jesus, but it is his presence, his compassion, his healing touch that will change your heart.

So what can we do to change our hearts? Two things. First, we can act as though we believe until experience begins to make us feel it. Our friends in the recovery movement have a saying, 'Fake it 'til you make it." Pretend you believe in the power of love even though you don't yet feel it. Try that new jack, even though it seems too fragile to lift your car. The first time I flew in a jumbo jet I had to pretend that I believed that that huge mass of metal could get off the ground. Even then it was some time before I put my full weight down.

Second, we can open ourselves to the love that can

touch us through others. God's love does not drop on us out of the sky. It touches us through the hands and voices of our family and our friends – or those who would be our friends if we would let them. We can allow ourselves to be touched by love, and our hearts will begin to change.

So what is this strange good news? Simply that all power and all love come from God and that that loving power is already ours for the asking. There is no way to guarantee security, no way to make people love you. But the power and love you need are already within you – the power to live, to face whatever life brings you, to give and to forgive; the love that you need to be healed, to be fed, to grow as a beloved son or daughter of a loving, divine Mother/Father. We are, each of us, invited to accept this simple gift of grace, and let it begin to turn us around.

THE LATE GEORGE TRAYLOR

It came at the end of my second year of Latin, when I was an earnest, bright fourteen year old at the Academy of Richmond County, a venerable, all male public high school in Augusta, Georgia. There were nine of us who struggled with Caesar and compared translations on the phone at night. Some were there because their doctor fathers told them to be there, others because they had doctor aspirations of their own and still believed the legend that doctors had to write their prescriptions in Latin. I had neither doctor parent nor doctor pretension. I was there simply because good students took Latin. And I was above all else expected to be a good student.

Perhaps he understood this better than I suspected, the quiet, patient, middle-aged man who was our teacher. Perhaps he saw this and more. At any rate, on the bottom of my final exam, Mr. Eubanks wrote two sentences that whisper to me after over fifty years:

"You are capable of doing great things – but it will probably be a good thing for you to fail at something along the way."

The first sentence lay upon me like a mantle, full of hope and heaviness. I felt a thrill at his vote of confidence, followed by the slightly sour aftertaste of weighty responsibility. But what of his strange final comment? What could he mean? How could he say such a thing? His paradoxical words seemed at once to set me up and cut me down.

Even now I wonder what Mr. Eubanks saw in that earnest, anxious boy. Perhaps he saw what I tried so carefully to conceal. Perhaps he was aware of the urgent, secret competitiveness that set me against anyone who might, by besting me academically, take away my one source of value, my stock in trade, my place of honor. Perhaps Mr. Eubanks had observed more carefully than I knew just how obsessively I had, for nine months now, labored to capture and deliver to the silent judges within me the prize held out to young men like me.

The George Traylor Memorial Medal was awarded each year to "the Academy sophomore of outstanding character and highest academic attainment." (No one could, I suppose, anticipate how the second of those requirements might play a part in corrupting the first.) No one could know how many times I wished I had never heard of George Traylor. Poor George, a lad long dead, honored by his parents with a medal aimed no doubt at encouraging other young men to do what their son had done. Neither he nor his parents could know how often I wished that George Traylor had never lived, or at least never died.

But maybe Mr. Eubanks did know. Maybe he wisely guessed how anxious I was about grades, how joyless was my pursuit of perfection, how silently my striving poisoned my feelings toward my nearest competitors. None of my fellow Latin students were threats for the medal. My enemy was Richard Woo*, a quiet and decent Chinese boy whose A's matched my own each report period. I could not speak to him or about him. I was sufficiently embarrassed by my obsession to keep it to myself. But perhaps it showed. Perhaps my teacher saw what my quest for the grail was doing to me and tried in his own gentle way to subvert my success for the sake of my soul.

I think that Mr. Eubanks saw me for who I was –tense, competitive, rigidly correct, far too concerned for recognition to have room for other things like friendship. I think that his subtle second sentence was an invitation to rejoin the human race. I think that he knew that his first sentence without the second would indeed be heard as a sentence – a life sentence – to someone who wished so desperately to win approval with his one talent.

I never spoke to my teacher about his cryptic and unnerving prescription. I never spoke to anyone else who might have helped me see in his riddle a word of grace. Even when, years later, the prescription was filled by moments of failure, I did not tip my hat to him for trying to warn me and prepare me.

Yes, I won the medal. And of course he was right.

* name has been changed

REDEMPTIVE IMAGINATION

You meant evil against me, but God meant it for good.
                                                    Genesis 50:20

A single event can appear very different to those who are there to see it. The meaning, we say, is in the eye of the beholder, whether that beholder be a person or a group or even a nation. After political candidates debate, their advisers meet immediately with the media to interpret the event, each to his own candidate's advantage. The media call this "spin."

Nations may put spin on events. The Book of Exodus tells of the liberation from Egypt of the Hebrew slaves, who were led by Moses who was led by God. My guess is that the Egyptian press reported the same event with a different spin, telling their shocked readers how a small mob of malcontents ran away from their rightful owners, disappearing into the swamps under cover of darkness, led by a fugitive from Egyptian justice.

Individuals put spin on the things that happen in their lives. I once knew a man and woman who decided to enlarge their family and share their home by adopting an infant from that category known as "Hard to Place." When their doctor asked if they were sure they were prepared for such a move, the husband replied, whether from ignorance or arrogance or blind faith, "We can handle it." Some years later the couple paused to reflect on the exhausting struggles of life with their adopted child. The father sighed, "Sometimes I wonder how we got ourselves into this." His wife replied, "Yes, but isn't it fortunate that we did. Her teenaged birth-parents might not have been able to give this child some of the care she needed."

One event. Two visions. One a weary lament sounding a lot like victimhood. The other a profoundly generous expression of grace. We might say that the mother had found a way to put a redemptive spin on what could otherwise have simply been seen as a tedious struggle. We will return to this story.

The story of Joseph and his brothers is one of the most beautiful biblical accounts of forgiveness and reconciliation. After surviving his brothers' treachery and spending years making a life and a name for himself in Egypt, Joseph finds himself in a position of power over them. He scares them a little by setting them up for possible prosecution But finally he rises above his sense of victimhood and his resentment and his thirst for revenge. He reveals himself to them. He embraces them. He even becomes the protector of their children.

How does Joseph do this? I call it an exercise in *redemptive imagination*. To put it simply, he asks himself one basic question: "Is there a better way to understand my story?" Certainly he could understand it as one justifying his deepest resentment. He is victim of a nasty plot, a plot causing him to spend years in exile far from his home. Certainly his brothers were jealous. And nasty. Except for the moderating influence of Reuben and Judah he would have died at their hands.

Joseph probably held on to this version of the story for some time. As a slave, as a prisoner, as an exile in a strange land, he certainly remembered his dream of domination and felt that his brothers had robbed him of that dream. But maybe somewhere along the way he began to ask a few more questions. What part did I play in this disaster? When I bragged about my dream and flaunted my robe, wasn't I provoking their jealousy? Was this simply a story of Good

Joseph and Bad Brothers? What about Jacob, whose favoritism had set me up? What about Reuben and Judah, who pleaded to spare me? I like to think that Joseph took what our friends in Alcoholics Anonymous call a "fearless moral inventory" to see just how he might have contributed to his own downfall. This is, I think, how to let go of victimhood and self-righteousness and revenge.

But he asked even more questions, questions that set his story in a wholly new frame. "Am I simply an unlucky exile," he may have asked, "or is there some way in which God wants me to be here?" And by the time Joseph had acquired power and found a way to use that power to save lives, he had also found a new way to understand his dream, his place in the family, his part in God's redemptive movement.

His brothers arrive searching desperately for food. Even after he has embraced them they are wary, wondering. how long his generosity will last. Maybe he is kind to them only for the sake of their father Jacob. What will happen when father is gone? Joseph offers them a new version of the old story. "I know," he says, "that you meant to do harm to me. But God meant it for good, to bring it about that many people should be kept alive. So do not fear; I will provide for you and your little ones."

We don't know exactly when Joseph finally became clear in this redemptive re-framing of his own story. Perhaps not until he actually saw his brothers on their knees before him and realized that his old dream was coming true in a way he had not anticipated. All we know is that he found a way to ask, "Is there another way to understand my story? Is there a better way to fulfill my old dream?" Because he was able to look at his story with eyes of faith, he was able to answer, "Yes."

All of us have the opportunity to be Joseph. All of us have the opportunity to ask the difficult questions that lead us beyond victimization and resentment; to understand our own story in new and redemptive ways. All it takes is honesty and imagination and faith.

First it takes honesty. Most of us are expert at finding a way to blame someone or something for everything that goes wrong in our lives. If we cannot identify a specific person to blame we can always fall back on the universal lament of the victim: "Life is not fair." Honesty requires that we look carefully and unflinchingly at the decisions we made, large and small, that contributed to our misfortunes. A "fearless moral inventory" requires that we be as clear about our own sins of omission and commission as we are about the sins of those around us. Even if we cannot identify any great failure, honesty should enable us to recall enough small flaws of character, enough moments of silent acquiescence, enough little lies to free us from the illusion of innocent victimhood. To be free from victimhood and the right to revenge is also to be free to find a better way to understand our story.

And that takes redemptive imagination. We can, if we are willing, ask the same question that I believe Joseph asked: "In what other way can I understand my story?" If I can no longer comfort myself with wounded innocence and dreams of revenge, how can I find something of value in my experience? If I no longer have the option of self-pity, how can I find in myself something of which to be proud? If I cannot think of myself as abandoned by God, how can I find a way to trust that I am being used by God?

That, of course, takes faith. Looking at life through the eyes of faith means trusting that God is present, even when our own vision is clouded by tears and our understanding distorted by anxiety, weariness and hurt. Looking at our own story through the eyes of faith means being willing to keep asking, "What good thing will God bring about for me and through me?"

The couple who looked back on life with their adopted child were asking these questions. "Why was it harder than we expected?" asked the father. "Were we a bit arrogant about our ability, a bit unrealistic about the hazards, a bit spoiled by earlier successes?" Honesty helped him past any permanent residence in the house of self-pity. The mother asked, "Is there another way to understand this story?" And she found one. Redemptive imagination helped her realize that, for all the struggle involved, they had been able to provide good care for a child who might otherwise not have received it. Finally, both were able to look at their story through eyes of faith. They were able to see that God had enriched their lives as well as that of their child. They knew that they were wiser, more compassionate, less likely to judge other struggling parents, more ready to admire the courage of those who overcome obstacles. Best of all, they knew that they had been blessed with the gift of love, laughter, beauty and grace that their "hard to place" child had brought into their lives.

The story of Joseph is our story, yours and mine. Or it can be. There is no story, however difficult, that cannot yield new meaning when we are willing to reflect on it with faithful redemptive imagination. There is no passage, however dark, that cannot be traveled with hopefulness. We have only to remind ourselves, "We are not alone. God is with us, helping us create something new."

PLAYGROUND PARABLE

I grew up before Little League. This means that I played my after-school baseball with no uniform, no regulation field, very little equipment and – perhaps most important – no adult supervision. The haphazard nature of equipment and field made little difference in the kind of game we played. The absence of fathers, coaches and umpires made a large difference.

Because there was no one to organize us, we had to work out our own version of parity on the spot every afternoon. A neighborhood game might begin with as many as a dozen players. Boys and girls. Big and little and mid-size. Since we could not assign different age groups to another league, we had to accommodate everyone on two teams and reach some kind of roughhewn equilibrium. Sometimes one team would be offered a couple of extra players. Depending on their age and skill, this might or might not be seen as an asset. If the larger and younger team still felt overmatched, its spokesman could ask for further concessions. The big boys might then volunteer to bat left-handed (except for the natural lefty, who also would switch to his weaker side). The younger kids might be offered other enticements, like an extra strike or even an extra out per inning. Thus did we negotiate until some grudging consensus was reached, with both teams loudly announcing that they were giving away the most.

Then there was the game itself, played without benefit of umpire. All of us knew and cherished the American tradition of umpire baiting. But how does one honor such a tradition when there is no umpire to bait? Or rather, when everyone on both teams (or at least those who are older and louder) volunteers as umpire in each critical moment? Yes, we baited each other. We screamed. We tortured logic, and each other, with pleas for justice and decency. "Admit you're wrong and we're right" was the basic burden of every argument.

When abuse, logic and appeals for justice failed, one side would abruptly resort to the Grand Gesture. "O.K., we'll give it to you. He's out." Then, in a wonderfully convoluted exercise in one-up-manship, the argument veered into a contest to see which side would emerge with the high moral ground and which would become the miserable recipient of charity. "No, we'll give it to you. Let him stay on second base. He's safe." The tone of the argument at this stage, while more restrained as befitted persons vying for the role of martyr, was no less intense. In fact it often seemed that the team winning the original dispute emerged the worse for the battle, with its base runner clinging shamefully to second base while his unselfish opponents played better baseball, inspired no doubt by the glow of their own virtue.

As for the lack of adult coaching, the vacuum again created opportunity for improvisation. More experienced players explained the rules to little brothers and sisters. Since no one could bear to watch while younger batters flailed vainly and violently at the ball, players from both teams shouted instruction: "Hold the bat higher." "Stand closer to the plate." "Swing!" Our coaching may have lacked in tact, but not in enthusiasm. We were even generous in our praise when a rookie finally connected.

Our field was a purist's nightmare. Home plate was a concrete slab about two feet from the wall of the elementary school, first base a metal railing surrounding a drain. Second base was an ill-defined low spot in the middle of the hard packed playground – hence the many arguments around second. Third base was a tree. Down the left field line ran a five foot wall, behind which was a rowhouse with wire mesh on its windows. Beyond the centerfield wall was Ellis Street. And right across the street from the playground was the front yard and garden of an extremely touchy older lady who did not hesitate to call the police when a ball, followed by an anxious young fielder, strayed into her yard. Perhaps it is understandable that one of our most important ground rules was: "Over the fence is out."

I have often watched and envied the children of Little League. Especially I am glad that they have the benefit of time and coaching from caring adults. But I also cherish what I learned in my pre-Little League youth. We were forced to learn many skills fit for the real world: how to achieve a balance of power among those of unequal assets, how to win an advantage while losing an argument, how to put aside competition long enough to show compassion, and how to hit to right field instead of swinging for the fence.

BUT WILL IT HOLD WATER?

My people have forsaken me, the fountain of living waters, and hewed out cisterns for themselves, broken cisterns that can hold no water.

Jeremiah 2:13

Like most of the rest of you I have my morning rituals that help me greet the day. Some, like coffee and shower, help me feel awake again. Others, like the more or less cheery greeting to my wife – then to my daughter and grandchildren when they arrive – are my way of reconnecting to the world of persons after my nightly voyage into the private world of sleep.

As I think about Jeremiah and his word about cisterns, two other rituals come to mind. First, I think of how I check each morning to see whether my bonsai needs water. Because the dish in which it grows is very shallow and because the water drains out through two holes in the bottom, the bonsai does in fact nearly always need to be watered.

Second, even before coffee or shower, before bonsai or breakfast, I stagger outside to get the morning paper. As soon as my eyes can focus I take note of three pages. I look at the front page to see what the world has done while I left it unattended. I scan the market summary to see how my mutual fund is doing. I turn to the sports page to find out whether the Orioles won or lost. As much as I hate to say so, I must admit that my mood for the day is colored just a bit in one direction or another by what these three pages tell me.

Now it occurs to me that my reading the paper is a little like checking my bonsai for water, except that I am the one that needs watering. And it occurs to me that one reason I have to do it every day is that whatever these pieces of news do for me, they don't seem to hold much water.

In a moment I will try to show you what I mean.

The prophet Jeremiah has hard words for his people. They have gone after worthlessness and so themselves become worthless. They have changed gods, even though what they now worship are no gods. They have, he says, changed their glory for that which does not profit. He sums up his charge in these words:

"My people have committed two evils; they have forsaken me, the fountain of living waters, and hewed out cisterns for themselves, broken cisterns that can hold no water."

If Jeremiah were alive today I wonder what he would say to us, as a nation and as individuals. Would he raise similar charges at us – how we have spoiled the good land that God gave us, mishandled God's law, gone after things that do not profit? Would he have something to say to us about hewing out broken cisterns that hold no water?

Let me name a few of the cisterns that may be leaky. They are all right there in my morning paper ritual.

I

There is the cistern of knowledge. I read the front page because I want to know what is going on in the world. Nothing wrong with that. The thirst for knowledge motivates much that we do – reading, education, the whole enterprise that we call science (which, after all, is just a fancy name for knowledge).

Knowledge helps us function better in the world. As

someone has said, "knowledge is power." There is nothing wrong with our quest for knowledge unless we delude ourselves into thinking that knowledge alone is enough to remove all mystery and give our lives meaning. Some persons in our time have been so awed by science that they have made it a god, claiming that only that is real which can be observed or measured by the scientific method. Perhaps we are all sometimes seduced by the great accomplishments of science and technology into thinking that way. But that, as someone has said, is like saying that only those areas of the sky exist that are illuminated by a searchlight, so that a giant aircraft that flew outside the arc of the searchlight would simply not exist.

One profound misunderstanding of science is to think that the only real world is the world that can be observed in the scientific searchlight. And that misunderstanding leads to the unfortunate assumption that our lives can and must find their meaning only in this limited sphere of material reality.

When our thirst for certainty tempts us to think that our limited knowledge – based on what our five senses can name and number – takes in every dimension of reality, then surely we are drinking from a cistern that does not hold water.

II

There is the cistern of security. I check the stock market to see how much reserve I can count on. Nothing wrong with that. We save in various ways – we call them "securities" – to provide for retirement and for rainy days. We invest to take care of ourselves and those whom we love. A certain amount of money in the bank can even liberate us from anxiety and free us to become better and more generous persons.

But in our thirst for security we are tempted to put too much trust in the cistern of material things. And of course there never seems to be enough. We find it reassuring to put away a little bit more. And then more and more. And sometimes that "more and more" causes us to become more and more out of touch with the real world in which most of our brothers and sisters struggle, a world from which our cistern of security insulates us.

Security can be a good thing. But if we rely on material security to guarantee us a sense of serenity in a troubled, suffering, sometimes dangerous world, then we have hewn out a cistern that will not hold water.

III

There is the cistern of status. I check on the baseball scores to see whether my team has won or lost. Their success becomes my success, their losses are a loss for me. Following a ball team is a daily adventure in vicarious competition. Put in terms of cisterns, my concern for the Orioles represents all of our efforts to build ourselves up by achievement, to gain status in the eyes of others and perhaps, finally, ourselves.

What is wrong with that? Are we not supposed to do our best, to use our talents, to "be all that we can be" as the US Army ad puts it? Of course we are. Our talents, our potential, our very lives are God's gift to us, to be used to the fullest. There is certainly nothing wicked about enjoying the accomplishments of others whose athletic skills exceed our own.

But if by our achievements, our vicarious success, and our accumulation of credentials we think to establish our worth as persons, if we imagine that we will somehow become larger along with our reputations and our résumés, then we have staked our lives on a cistern that will not hold water. If we pin our hope on what Shakespeare called the "bubble reputation," we will find that our sense of self can be deflated along with the bubble.

So, these are our broken cisterns, cisterns into which we pour our hopes and dreams, wondering if they will hold water. We think that if we can only know enough, have enough, be enough our lives will have meaning and value.

We rely on the cistern of knowledge in the pleasant illusion that we can know enough, forgetting Paul's word that "we know in part and we prophecy in part." We put our faith in the cistern of security, persuading ourselves that we can have enough, and ignoring those uncomfortable old warnings about laying up treasures on earth. We are seduced by the cistern of status, convincing ourselves that all will be well with us if we can be enough, if only others will admire us and build us up. And then we are jarred by the words of Jesus: "everyone who exalts himself will be humbled; and he who humbles himself will be exalted."

What does he mean by that? Is Jesus saying that God is like a mean-spirited parent who doesn't want us to feel good about ourselves? Is his the kind of God who likes to knock down anyone whose head rises above the crowd?

I don't think that is his point. I think that Jesus is simply speaking of the way things are. He is describing what we might call a law of spiritual growth. Those who try to build themselves up find themselves shrinking, while those who give themselves away become larger persons. As someone has said, the smallest package is the man who is wrapped up in himself. John Donne was right when he wrote that "each man's death diminishes me." But the reverse is also true. Each person's life and love enlarge me, and they enlarge the one whose life is lived in love.

IV

Walking to Wisdom

Let me tell you about a man who played a very important part in my life. His name was John.

John was a brilliant engineer. He worked in experimental television a dozen years before anyone ever met Howdy Doody. He played an important role in developing radar during World War II. On many visits to our home he turned his engineering gift to the practical task of repairing anything electronic that moved – or rather that failed to move as it should.

John had a great deal of knowledge but he also knew that there was a reality beyond what he could know. He had a comfortably secure lifestyle, but he was able to share what he had rather than try to accumulate more. He was held in high esteem by his scientific colleagues for his professional accomplishments and by his friends for his practical skills, yet he was an unfailingly modest, soft-spoken man for whom the word "humble" comes quickly to mind.

I admired John for his knowledge, enjoyed being a guest in his well-ordered home, was well aware of his reputation. But what enlarged him in my eyes and my heart and my memory was his gift of himself. What made him a big man was the generous way he gave his time and energy and friendship to those whose lives he touched.

John has a special place in my life because of the kind of man he was and because I married his only daughter. I have been enlarged by knowing him. And I continue to be enlarged as I experience his loving spirit being lived out in the daughter who is so like him in so many ways.

The word of Jeremiah challenges us to test the vessels in which we try to preserve meaning, worth or hope. He reminds us that knowledge and security and status are good gifts of God but that none of them alone hold the water that gives life.

The word of Jesus points us toward a simple truth

about spiritual growth. He reminds us that love is the gift that enlarges both the one who gives and the one who receives; that the only way to become larger is to give oneself away; that the only vessel that finally holds water is the cup with which we share ourselves with those who need us.

DEATH OF A HUNTER

We developed a strange ritual, Billy and I. When we succeeded, over considerable odds, in actually shooting one of the birds on my Father's unendangered list, we conducted a solemn funeral. I was eleven or twelve, my Cousin Billy a year older. We spent a lot of summer days at the South Georgia farm of our Aunt Ellamae. We were allowed to shoot at birds with a .22 caliber rifle. My father doled out a few bullets at a time, along with clear and rigid instructions about where we could shoot, what we could shoot, and how much we could shoot.

We could only shoot at birds that were in trees or on telephone lines; never must we be caught aiming the rifle in a horizontal plane except to fire at tin cans propped against the side of the barn. Haunted by visions of patrol cars coming to tell us of a hunter found dead in some nearby woods, the victim of one of my stray horizontal bullets, I found it easy to obey that particular rule even though it often eliminated some of the more tempting targets that perched in the hedges and fig trees that surrounded the house. Another rule involved what we could shoot. Long before Harper Lee's novel, we learned that it was a sin to kill a Mockingbird. The Brown Thrasher was the State Bird and also off limits. Likewise Bluebirds, Cardinals, and Robins, protected either by law or by my father's own personal edict. In fact, about the only birds likely to fall victim to our deadly stalking were the jumpy targets called Sparrows and those despised invaders known as Starlings. We became as expert in identifying fair game as we were at naming the silhouettes of the fighter planes that were flying over Europe and the Pacific at the same time that we carried on our private war in rural Georgia.

The funerals were, I think, a way of relieving our guilt when we finally downed a Sparrow and retrieved it from the tall grass. We were not hunting for food, only for sport. There was nothing to do with our victim after the first excitement of watching it fall. It seemed only fair to give the birds a decent burial, since the birds had given us, at some cost to themselves, a moment of triumph. From the kitchen we brought small jars to serve as coffins. We buried the jars in a row, and Billy thoughtfully added flowers on each tiny grave.

Our little killing field grew slowly. The birds were not, in fact, in great danger from our assaults, since we were barely able to hold the rifle still without finding a tree or a fence to help out. And the body of a Sparrow makes an exceedingly small target. Still we persisted, roaming over the farmyard and down the nearby roads. Billy's excited battle cry still rings in my memory: "Yonder sets a bird on that wire!"

One day hunting season came to an abrupt halt, never to resume. There was nothing unusual about the day or the kill, although the bird that I felled was not the usual Sparrow or Starling but an equally tiny Wren, a bird whose distinctive long tail feathers let me know that I had scored a special hit. I searched in the grass beneath the pecan tree until I found the small clump of feathers. The Wren's head had been taken off cleanly. There was no blood or broken wing, indeed no sign that the bird had ever possessed a head. Something about that tiny decapitated creature made me feel slightly sick somewhere within, somewhere deeper than my queasy stomach. We had our funeral, but my heart was not in it. Billy tried to continue the hunt, but I had no taste for it. I never shot a bird again. Something about the death of a Wren led to the death of a hunter as well.

THE ULTIMATE POWER TRIP

He disarmed the principalities and powers and made a public example of them...

Colossians 2:15

For most of my life I have loved stories about ships. One of my childhood favorites was *Treasure Island.* I learned about England's sea war with Napoleon through the adventures of Captain Horatio Hornblower and tasted the navy of World War II in *Mr. Roberts* and *The Caine Mutiny.* I dreamed a lot about going to sea. Well, I had the chance to give my fantasies a reality check. I was invited to go along on a one day destroyer cruise from the U.S. Naval Station at Norfolk. It was a good day. An eye-opening day. An exhausting day. A day filled with disturbing questions and conflicting feelings. Let me name just a few:

I felt an exhilarating sense of speed, freedom, and power as we headed out of the Chesapeake Bay. I felt awe at the size of this "small" gunship and admiration for the skill and competence of the crew. I felt pride in their obvious discipline and dedication and fascination as they showed us the missile silos and talked about smart torpedoes. I even felt – along with the crew – a bit of a power trip when the drawbridge opened to let us pass, and all those cars had to wait for us.

I listened as an enthusiastic young woman, a graduate of the Naval Academy, told us of her duties as a gunnery officer, and found my admiration and fascination clouded over with a deep sadness. Please understand. I had no question of her right to serve, no doubts about her competence or her personal moral character. But I was sad just the same – sad that even as we have progressed to the point where our daughters are free to pursue careers that were formerly closed to them, even now, after two thousand years of Christian civilization, we as a people are still investing much of our treasure, our energy, our creativity in building bigger and better war machines, still teaching and equipping and inspiring fine young men and women to become professional gunners.

I have thought a lot about that scene on board the destroyer. I have wondered how – and even whether – to give voice to the concerns it raised in me. Perhaps, I thought, perhaps in the world as it is such an investment in the power to dominate and destroy is somehow a necessary evil. But even as I comforted myself with that thought, I could not get away from other thoughts. Can we not at least wonder whether we have justified our addiction to certain ideas about power and violence by wrapping our weapons of destruction in flags of glory, whether we have not somehow refused to take seriously the full impact of the Christian gospel?

My day on the destroyer raised some disturbing questions – questions about the way we as Christians think and live. Does power really corrupt, or do we corrupt power? Is violence really redemptive, or do we justify it to avoid facing something in ourselves? Is there a better way that we are afraid to try? I want to offer my own answers to these three questions. What I have to say may annoy you. You may want to take issue with me. I hope that you will. I want to challenge some of your – and my – favorite assumptions. I want us to look for new possibilities.

I

I believe that we have redefined power to suit our wish

to be in control. We like to think that having power means being in charge – not just of ourselves but of other people. If I have power I can make other people do it my way. We persist in thinking this way even though we know that this kind of abuse of power eventually leads to what we call a power struggle.

We know that governments who abuse their power over the people invite revolution; we know that corporations who try to control people with economic power produce a backlash of strikes and government intervention. We watch parents exercise too much power over their children, and we are not surprised when they find themselves dealing with runaways, rebels or dropouts. We even observe how churches try to control the thoughts and actions of their members, only to find themselves faced with what those in power call "heresy" and those not in power call "reform."

We shake our heads and sadly quote that famous maxim: "Power corrupts." It is almost as though we are saying that we are really nice folks until this bad thing called power comes along and corrupts us. *But I think it is not power that corrupts us. I think it is we who corrupt power.*

Power, after all, is a gift of God. It is not in itself a corrupt thing. What we all know and prefer to forget is that human beings tend to have a distorted view of their place in the scheme of things. Human beings want to be owners rather than trustees, bosses rather than partners, rivals rather than brothers and sisters. This is, I have to say, what we mean when we speak of the original sin – this tendency to try to rearrange the divine order of things so as to place ourselves near the top of the heap. It is what Christian theologians for two thousand years have understood as humanity's fallen nature. Power is not bad. Neither are human beings. But human beings are fallen, and so they tend to distort, abuse, corrupt something that was intended as God's good gift.

Let's face it. There is something very beguiling about power. That is why we call it a "power trip." What we must ask ourselves is whether this trip, like other trips, is at bottom an addiction. Is it, like all addictions, one more way that we try to fill the empty space and prove that we are who we pretend to be?

We have said that every abuse of power leads to struggle and reaction. What is worse, most reactions lead to new abuse. So revolutions often lead to abuse of power by the revolutionaries; sons run away from abusive fathers only to grow up and become abusive fathers to their sons; schismatic churchmen create new and oppressive orthodoxies. It is not that there is something wrong with power. But there is something terribly wrong with the way we think about it.

II

We have convinced ourselves that violence is redemptive as a way of justifying our own violent inclinations. Rev. Pat Robertson felt obliged to warn the folks in Florida that God just might send a hurricane, or even terrorists, to punish them for their Disney-like departures from the one and only way (which, I gather, is "Pat Robertson's way"). I found myself wondering whether these promised disasters were really God's method of punishment or rather Pat Robertson's way of baptizing his own anger. Was this modern prophet really speaking the word of the Lord or was he projecting onto God his own wish to do violence to those with whom he disagreed?

Someone has called it the *Myth of Redemptive Violence*. It has been around so long that we almost take it as a given. We tell ourselves that a certain amount of violence is really a good thing because it makes people better. "Just one more war will bring in the kingdom of the Prince of Peace." "Just one more hanging will make the bad people good – or at least scare them into behaving." "Just one more beating will make my child kind and loveable and respectful."

And deep inside us we know it isn't so. Overwhelming research tells us that abusers were themselves abused. Our own experience as individuals and as a nation reminds us that violence begets violence. And of course there is the quiet voice of Jesus in the garden speaking to Peter – and across the centuries to us, a voice that says, "they that live by the sword shall perish by the sword."

A question for us all. Do we cling to the myth of redemptive violence because it is true? Or because we are unready to hear and learn and risk a better way?

III

We have avoided facing the clear message of the New Testament about the true meaning of power. The bad news is that fallen human beings – that means us – have corrupted power by our stubborn insistence on using it in our own fashion. The good news is that there is a better way, in fact a divine way. That way is no mystery. It shouts from every page of the New Testament.

In our text for today Paul proclaims that Jesus has "disarmed all the principalities and powers." How? Not by coercion. Jesus never coerced anyone. Not by violence. Jesus did not imitate the violence of the powers of the world; he overcame their violence by absorbing its fury into himself. The Jesus that I meet in the New Testament consistently challenges our idea of power as control; he consistently takes on every person and every institution that uses power to control other human beings – through government, or wealth, or religion, or family tradition.

The Jesus that I meet in the New Testament leads us, I believe, toward a radically new understanding of power. He leads us to think of power not as domination but as energy, not as violence but as vitality, not as the capacity to control but as the capacity to create. The divine power that comes to its fullest human expression in Jesus is not a power over other people but a power within oneself.

But this power that Jesus lives out is still something that we are afraid to grasp after two thousand years. We prefer our own version. We want to be in charge. We still reward those who seem to be in charge with our admiration. Or is it our envy? Or perhaps our fear? But let us not comfort ourselves that the power we admire so much is God's kind of power.

Long before Jesus' day the prophet Hosea told his people that God's power is both gentler and greater than humanity's distorted understanding. When the prophet spoke to Israel of how God continued to reach out to His people even when they were unfaithful, he put it this way:

I will not execute my fierce anger, I will not destroy Ephraim; for I am God and not man, the Holy One in your midst, and I will not come to destroy.

The good news of Christ invites us to entrust ourselves to God for the ultimate power trip. It won't make drawbridges open, but it may help us build bridges to our brothers and sisters. It won't give us the satisfaction of controlling anyone – except perhaps ourselves. But it may open our spirits to the deepest wells of creative energy within us. And maybe, just maybe, that will be enough.

THE PASTOR AND THE RELIGIOUS FANATIC

"A fanatic," says Nicolai Berdyaev, "is a person who can think of only one thing at a time." The Russian theologian, who calls fanaticism a "painful distortion of conscience," puts his finger on a central weakness in this person whom all pastors know, some pastors admire, and many pastors dread.

Fanaticism is always religious, at least in the sense that the fanatic always elevates something or someone to the level of absolute. The very word comes from the Latin word for temple (*fanum*) and was first used to denote an enthusiastic prophet. So what, we need to ask ourselves, is eating the religious fanatic? And what can we do with him, or for her?

Berdyaev points toward an understanding. A fanatic is a person grasping for simple answers to complex questions. Out of idealism or frustration or narrowed vision the fanatic stakes her life – and even the lives of others – on her special set of absolutes. A fanatic is a human being like the rest of us who is trying to make his way in the world by reducing to manageable proportions the wonderful and bewildering complexity of that world. All of us would like a glimpse of divine wisdom, a sense of divine presence, a share in divine power. In our limited knowledge and terrifying aloneness and humbling frailty such wisdom and presence and power is something for which we are hungry. So we grasp at a holy book, defend our holy places, claim for our movement a holy destiny. And those who claim another book, another place, another destiny? They become the enemy, the outsider, the infidel. Not only because they do not share our vision but because their very claim threatens the absolute validity of ours.

All of us have known fanatics. We have probably envied them their certainty. We have felt the pull within ourselves to wipe out complexity and ambivalence with a wave of our chosen banner.

What can a pastor do in the face of this understandable but frightening response to such a deep human need? Four suggestions. Because the fanatic has often experienced frustration or even what he may think of as failure in some sphere of his life, it is helpful to encourage him in the direction of some creative act – as simple as planting a garden or as challenging as learning to play a musical instrument. Eric Hoffer has observed that extreme poverty does not seem to lead to fanaticism for those who are constantly renewing their sense of worth through creative work. "Nothing so bolsters our self-confidence and reconciles us with ourselves," he writes, "as the continuous ability to create; to see things grow and develop under our hand, day in, day out."

Second, as the fanatic begins to discover the value of creativity for herself, encourage her to grant that same freedom to others. Berdyaev makes an eloquent plea for a tolerance which is rooted in the "tolerance of God for human freedom, even the freedom to do evil." Respect for another's freedom to think and act differently from what I desire is another name for tolerance. Call it the willingness to live with the ambiguity that goes with human freedom.

Third, since the religious fanatic is constantly searching for absolutes, try to point him gently in the direction of guiding principles rather than absolute practices, rituals or even beliefs. Gandhi and Martin Luther King, Jr., two men who might have been called fanatics, managed to temper their vision and harness into creative paths the explosive energies of their followers by adhering to a single principle – the principle of non-violence. Honoring such a guiding principle can help tame and channel the fanatic spirit.

Finally, though, the pastor's greatest hope is to help the person gripped by fanaticism to experience for himself the *only* Absolute, the One who alone is God. Not ideas about God or particular rituals or practices of those who seek God, but God only. At the heart of that experience of the Absolute all names and rules and books and places become clearly something *less* than absolute. To encourage persons toward the experience of God is the pastor's ultimate goal.

WHEN YOUR CUP OVERFLOWS

...then Samuel took the horn of oil, and anointed him in the presence of his brothers; and the Spirit of the Lord came mightily upon David from that day forward.
I Samuel 16:13

...thou anointest my head with oil; my cup runneth over.
Psalm 23

We all know that the good looking little brother goes on to become the king's protégé and music therapist, that he makes a name for himself as war hero and finally becomes the founder of a dynasty. We also know that tradition has it that the golden boy who becomes king is also a golden singer who gave us the words of everyone's favorite psalm, the one that says "thou anointest my head with oil; my cup runneth over."

When I think about David's career and listen to his psalm I'm tempted to say, "Sure, David, easy for you to say that God anoints you. You *were* God's anointed. Easy to say that your cup runneth over; your whole life was filled to overflowing with good things."

Then I remind myself that the cup from which David drank was not always sweet, that the overflow sometimes left stains. I remind myself that the little boy with beautiful eyes was also the one assigned to stay out with the sheep and protect them from wild beasts, that the young court favorite was almost killed by the jealous king. I remember that the powerful head of state was confronted and shamed by the prophet Nathan when he had violated the marriage

Walking to Wisdom

of Bathsheba and used his power to see that her husband was killed. I remember that the founder of a dynasty had to deal with a son who led an armed rebellion against his father, that, even so, he mourned when that son, Absalom, was killed against David's orders by his Chief of Staff.

In some ways David and his overflowing cup seem larger than life. But in other ways his life is very much like ours, and his cup of blessing is not so different from ours. Think with me about our overflowing cups and how we deal with them.

Sometimes when our cup overflows we don't even notice how full it is. A friend reminded me that having leftovers in the refrigerator is evidence of an overflowing cup. Many folks, after all, are not sure from one meal to the next whether there will be enough to go around. So leftovers are unnoticed evidence of an overflowing cup. So is the old used car we keep, the one that needs a few extra trips to the garage. So is the old computer that just doesn't function as quickly as the newer models. So is the attic full of extra furniture, clothing, books, gadgets and toys that seem like a burden when it is time to move. Next time you start to complain about the leftovers in your life remind yourself that your cup is overflowing.

Sometimes when our cup overflows we feel overwhelmed. At those times we usually don't say that our cup is overflowing but rather that "our plate is full." We have too many meetings on our schedule, too much house to take care of, too many activities to drive our children to. We shake our heads at the number of choices on cable TV, the variety of brands in the supermarket, the dizzying number of entertainment options on any given weekend. We literally long for a time and place where we can "get away from it all" and by "it" we mean the overload of blessings that fill our plates and our cups to overflowing.

And, of course, *sometimes when our cup overflows we*

have to deal with the stains. Not all full cups taste sweet. Not all blessings are recognized as blessings until later, often much later. Most of us, looking back, can see that a certain failure opened a door to growth, that a painful divorce led to a new and better relationship, that a disappointment in work or school led us to find a new path or a new strength. Most of us have discovered along the way that a painful, even bitter tasting, cup has taught us more about loving than a sweet one. David suffered the loss of his friend Jonathan but somehow became more compassionate toward Jonathan's father Saul. He was humiliated by Nathan and perhaps in the process learned forgiveness for his son Absalom.

So, what can we say about our overflowing cups? Three words. Be alert. Be patient. Be generous.

Be alert. When you have leftovers, remember that leftovers come from an overflowing cup. When you feel overwhelmed, remind yourself that your sense of overload is directly related to the tremendous overflow with which your life is blessed.

Be patient. Don't be too quick to throw out the bitter tasting wine or too ready to curse the occasional stain. Give yourself time to grieve your losses and heal your hurts, then ask yourself whether even this bitter cup may carry an opportunity for deeper understanding. Don't let the bitter taste of the cup flavor your outlook on life.

Be generous. When you realize that your cup is overflowing, start spreading it around. When your closet overflows, give away some clothes. When your bank account overflows, give away some money. When blessings overflow, share a blessing. Just as it is sometimes hard for us to recognize blessings, it also seems hard to give them to others. This is a puzzling thing. When the world is so hungry, why do we hoard our food? When those close to us are hungry for praise or encouragement, why are we so stingy with life-giving words?

Maybe we are misled by their show of self-sufficiency, so we think that they don't need our encouragement. Or maybe we feel we have nothing to give. I think that sometimes we operate out of a sense of our own poverty, so that we don't think that our words or our gifts are of much worth to anyone else. Or perhaps we think that people must do something special to earn our blessing (just as we believe we must do something to deserve notice from others). It doesn't occur to us to admire people for making the most of life within their limitations; to praise children for holding their own in a disagreement; to compliment those who have the courage to leave a degrading job or others who hang on in a difficult situation instead of giving up.

We tend, in short, to praise people for extraordinary things and to overlook those who desperately need our blessing just for struggling to be themselves. Robert Bly, speaking of the needs of young men, said it this way: "Any young man who is not being admired by an older man is being hurt." He is saying the truth – and not just for the young or just for men.

There are men and women, old and young, who are hungry for what you have to give, people who are closer than you imagine. If you hold back because you yourself feel impoverished or because you are waiting for them to do something special, then everyone will be the poorer. They will stay hungry and you will miss your chance to share from your overflowing cup.

Just do it. Tell them something you admire about them. It will make their day and yours too. If you can't think of anything to admire, think harder; you need some exercise in compassionate imagination. Or ask them to do you a favor. Asking people a favor lets people know that you value them and what they have to give. At the end of Steinbeck's

Walking to Wisdom

East of Eden, the rebellious Cal is seeking his dying father's blessing. Cal's friend Abra pleads with the old man: *"You have to let him know that you love him. Ask him for something. Let him do for you!"*

The best thing we can do with the overflow of blessing we have received from God is to share it. Don't be shy. Don't be embarrassed. Don't be stingy. Life is too short and the world is too hungry.

KILLERS OF THE WHINE

Two of my favorite people long ago consorted to destroy one of my favorite pastimes. I am sure they held no malice against me. They were, I suspect, only expressing their own preference or, at worst, protecting themselves from fallout. Certainly they did not conspire to commit their deed, nor co-ordinate their attack for maximum impact. I doubt either realized the power of her words or the common front they presented, although I know that they admired and respected each other and would certainly have applauded had they witnessed the other in action.

At the time of her assault, Elizabeth was in her late eighties, a lively widow who had in her earlier years presided over the middle school at Sidwell Friends School in Washington, D.C. In retirement she was active in founding the new Presbyterian church to which I had been called as organizing pastor. Elizabeth's attitude toward life and its rocky curves can best be captured by her report to me on moving into a retirement community at the age of ninety. "Why, David," she announced, "it's just like going off to college. So many new people to meet!" Elizabeth found a way to taste every flavor that life offered. But she had little time, as I discovered, for dwelling on that which was sour.

The day of our encounter was hot and steamy, even in our pleasant little Virginia village with a view of the Blue Ridge. Elizabeth answered my knock and welcomed me into the neat new home that she and Charles had built a few years before his death. They had not troubled themselves to include air-conditioning.

After the custom of summertime small talk I began to comment on the oppressive heat that had followed me on my afternoon calls. I had hardly begun to elaborate on the awfulness of the day when Elizabeth interrupted me in her cheerfully assertive way. "You know," she laughed, "I've never seen much point in complaining about the weather. We can't do anything about it anyway." I was cut off in mid-whine. The conversation immediately turned to other, more edifying topics, as I silently reminded myself, "Never complain about the weather around Elizabeth."

At the time that she collaborated with Elizabeth in destroying my pastime, my daughter Ellen was about seventeen, an energetic young woman who was infected early with much of Elizabeth's genius for finding the best flavors in whatever life asked her to taste. One of the loves that she shared with me was baseball. She had become, like her father, a devoted Orioles fan, her genuine fondness for the game being enriched by the opportunity to fantasize about a young Oriole named Cal Ripken, Jr., at that time a highly eligible bachelor with bright blue eyes, an engaging manner and an attitude toward his work that Ellen admired.

We liked to go to ball games together, even though the drive from northern Virginia to Baltimore took nearly two hours and made each game seem a major league investment in time and energy. It was on one of our Orioles trips that Ellen delivered the second punch of the one-two combination begun by Elizabeth in her living room some years earlier.

The Yankees were in town. The Yankees, against whom I had held a grudge since 1949 when they defeated my Red Sox on the last day of the season. We had hardly settled into our upper deck seats in Memorial Stadium when the blows began to fall. We sat in stunned silence as the Yankees scored nine runs in the first inning.

I was disgusted. I was morose. I whined aloud about every bloop hit and faulty piece of umpiring that had played a part in that nine run debacle. I groaned with dread at the prospect of a long losing afternoon in the hot sun. I resented the four hours we would spend in the car. Having been deprived of the pleasure of watching a winning – or at least a close – ball game, I had settled into an alternative pleasure. I was now savoring the sweet misery of complaint.

Ellen put up with me for awhile. Then, in the middle of the third inning, she made her move. "Dad, if you don't stop complaining I'm going to sit somewhere else. We came all the way up here to see a ball game and I want to enjoy it." My grousing subsided to a few sullen mutters. For a long time we sat in silence. Ellen cheered what there was to cheer about, and I eventually joined her. The Orioles lost to the hated Yankees. I lost something too. Never again would I feel free to complain at a ball game with complete abandon.

I would not say that Elizabeth and Ellen completely killed my ability to whine. I am made of sturdier stuff than that. But they certainly haunt me, both of them, when I indulge myself too much. They remind me that life has too many good flavors to linger long on bitterness.

CASTLES IN THE SAND

Everyone who hears these words of mine and does not act on them will be like a foolish man who built his house on sand.

Matthew 7:26

When I graduated from seventh grade quite a few years ago, one of the memorable moments for me was the recitation of a poem by one of my classmates. It was memorable for two reasons. First I remember how terrified he looked as he gave his sweaty and sing-song rendition of Rudyard Kipling's collection of sage advice called *If.* Second, I remember the whole poem, having listened to him recite it at endless rehearsals. I will not favor you with the whole thing; but I want to share one of the couplets that stuck with me and still catches my attention. Perhaps you remember it too:

If you can meet with triumph and disaster,
And treat those two imposters just the same.

What, I have asked myself from time to time, did he mean by that? Are they really imposters, triumph and disaster? And how in the world can I treat them the same? Kipling was not the only one who suggested such a thing. No less a thinker than St. Paul tells us, "I know how to be abased and I know how to abound." There you are, triumph and disaster. Paul doesn't call them imposters, but he does apparently treat them the same.

Why does the poet call them "imposters"? Because

they pretend to be more than they are. Because both can lead us to wrong conclusions about ourselves and about life and about God. Let me try to show you what I mean by taking a careful look at the little story with which Jesus ends his Sermon on the Mount.

Jesus tells us about those who build castles on the sand. The point of his story is plain enough. Lives that are built on shaky foundations are, sooner or later, going to fall. The picture of the crumbling castle is certainly a picture of disaster; and we can all think of some castles in our own time: beach houses undermined by hurricanes; Enron-shaped castles collapsing on their shaky accounting foundations; quiet households suddenly shattered by cancer, alcohol, unemployment, divorce. It is not hard to see how disaster can threaten our castles.

But what about the castles that don't collapse? What about mansions built on sand that the hurricanes miss? What about generations of castle builders who, by reason of good fortune and good management, keep their sand castles intact? How will they discover that even their triumphs may be imposters, that their foundations are not sound? It seems to me that both castles that collapse and castles that don't collapse can lead us into temptation.

I

It is not hard to see how disasters threaten us. Let me name just a few. There is natural disaster: the unearned and unexpected misfortunes of life, sickness, accident, the death of a loved one. There is relationship disaster: the hurt we suffer at the hands of others, rejection, betrayal, abuse, neglect. There is personal disaster: the pain we bring upon ourselves through misjudgment, self-defeating habit or unwise choices.

How are these disasters a threat to us? Obviously they

threaten our health, our security, our chances for happiness. We have all, at some time, had to deal with such disasters; we all bear scars inflicted by life, by other people, by our own failures. But the worst hurt that disaster can do to us is the hurt to our spirit. Natural disaster can turn you against God; betrayal or abuse can turn you against people; failure can turn you against yourself. If sickness or loss has led you to feel that life is empty and God uncaring, if you have been hurt or rejected and said to yourself, "people can't be trusted," if you have known failure and have given up on yourself – then disaster has done its worst to you.

But what if Kipling is right? What if disaster really is an imposter? Perhaps natural disaster is only an accident of nature, one of the ragged edges of a good creation. Maybe the hurt you suffered at the hands of others came simply from the weakness of those particular people and is not reason enough to say that people are no damn good. And what if your failures are only stumbles on a long and rocky path, not the final proof that your whole life is wasted? *Having* a failure does not *make* you a failure, you know. It is only a single measure of your doing, not of your being.

So, how is disaster an imposter? Because it pretends that the bad things that happen prove that life is bad. It tempts us to lose faith in God and in other people and in ourselves. And that is an illusion, a terribly destructive illusion. For me, disaster is not the meaning of the opera; it is only a discordant note in the music.

II

But what about triumph? How can triumph harm us? What may happen to those whose castles survive intact? We all hear that success is dangerous, that success can cause people to forget their friends, to lose their sense of humanity, to presume that they are wiser or better than they really are. Triumph endangers our spirits in the opposite way from disaster. Where disaster can make us bitter and despairing, triumph can make us prideful and shallow, presuming to think that our good fortune is our just reward. It can tempt us to think that we are "self-made" men or women or, if we have saved a place for faith in our lives, we may think along the lines of the bumper sticker I saw recently that said, "Jesus loves all of us, but I'm one of his favorites." Triumph can do more harm to our spirits than disaster, for pain is a better soil for growth than pleasure, and such things as compassion and forgiveness are usually born of suffering.

But triumph too is an imposter, for the same reason that disaster is. Triumph tempts us to think that external achievements – wealth, success, recognition – are a measure of internal worth. It supposes that doing is more important than being, that expensive garments can conceal an empty heart. It may in fact be harder to deal with triumph than with disaster, as Jesus reminds us when he says that a camel can get through a needle's eye easier than rich folks through the gates of heaven. Why is this so? Because triumphs, and the power that comes with them, tend to corrupt our hearts. Robert E. Lee once observed that slavery was "more tragic, perhaps, for master than for slave." Simone Weil wrote that "force is as pitiless to the man who possesses it as it is to its victims; the second it crushes, the first it intoxicates."

Why is the arrogance born of triumph more dangerous than the despair born of disaster? Perhaps because we are more ready to be saved from our despair than from our arrogance. Why are triumph and disaster both imposters? Because they both tempt us to trust the wrong foundations, to measure our worth by external standards and the goodness of God by the size of our bank account.

How can we treat these two imposters the same? By

reminding ourselves that we are founded and grounded in the love of God, and not in anything we do or fail to do; that disaster does not mean that God loves us less; that triumph does not mean that God loves us more. William Sloane Coffin said it this way:

> *God's love doesn't seek value, it creates value. It is not because we have value that we are loved; it is because we are loved that we have value. Our value is a gift, not an achievement . . .so we do not have to prove ourselves, only express ourselves, and what a world of difference there is between proving ourselves and expressing ourselves.*

I believe that it is upon the rock solid foundation of God's love that we can build our castles, our lives, our best hopes; that we can express ourselves as fully and as faithfully as we are able, knowing that we are rooted and grounded in a God who loves us and never lets us go.

PREJUDICE

When my parents told me we were moving to Atlanta, I felt a deep shock of fear. I had just finished first grade when I learned that the railroad was transferring my father to its Atlanta office. Most of my feelings I can only guess at. I suppose I was sad, since Fort Lauderdale was the only home I had known. I was probably excited about the summer because we would be staying on our grandparents' farm as long as possible, to avoid something called polio that threatened in the places where other children were close at hand. And I think that I caught a little of my parents' pleasure at moving closer to their families in Georgia. I'm sure I was relieved that I would be spared the long car-sick journeys from south Florida.

But the only feeling I clearly remember when I heard the word "Atlanta" was fear. "That," I told myself, "is where mean people live." Since I told only myself and no one else of this deeply held conviction, I continued to carry it with me for years, yielding my prejudice only as new experience and new evidence transformed my image of the city and its people.

My fear of Atlanta, like many fears, was born of a disturbing experience that was first distorted and then exaggerated. It began and ended with a single harrowing incident in a train station that left an Atlanta-shaped stain on my young mind.

The trip was an exciting one for me, although I'm sure my mother could not have relished traveling alone from Florida to Indiana with two small children. My brother Danny was about six; I was two years younger. We were on our way to Indiana to visit Ibbie, my mother's lovable older sister and my favorite aunt by far. Because our father worked for the railroad we were traveling on a pass. I loved the Pullman car, a place of wonder where beds appeared from the wall and people struggled to dress behind the curtains that lined the swaying aisle. I can still feel the excitement of a night on the sleeper where no one really slept. That is a memory unstained by the incident in Atlanta.

I suppose we were changing trains in Atlanta's Terminal Station. I remember following my mother as she hurried down the platform trying to catch up with the conductor. For some obscure and probably legitimate reason he had not returned my mother's annual pass after taking it up on the train, and she was beginning to fear that we would be leaving the station without it. When she tried to get his attention on the noisy platform, he was short with her, turning her anxiety into anger. For a young woman in a strange place halfway between a husband in Florida and a sister in Indiana, losing her pass must have felt like losing one's lifejacket on an ocean liner. And losing it to a short-tempered, red-faced, officious old man in a uniform had pushed her close to screaming hysteria.

I was anxious with her anxiety. I was angry at the man who first ignored, then spoke sharply to my mother. I knew nothing of the mysterious ways of railroad conductors. I only knew that we were in a big noisy building in a place called Atlanta and a mean man was making my mother cry.

My prejudice lingered with me for years. Even after we were settled happily in Atlanta's suburbs I was anxious about trips downtown. Even when Ibbie moved from Indiana to Atlanta and we visited her house I was uneasy about meeting her neighbors. In short, I remained convinced that Atlanta was hostile territory. My conviction was based on a single experience with a single person who *very likely was passing through the city just as we were. I was not personally threatened. Nor, in all probability, was my mother. She was anxious and alone, trying to deal with a man who was tired and harried.*

My prejudice, like most prejudice, was the product of limited exposure, distorted perceptions, unvalidated assumptions and unreasoning fear. It was not until I fell in love with baseball and the Atlanta Crackers that I began to forgive the city, and not until I discovered and absorbed the saga of Scarlett O'Hara that I learned to like it.

WHAT ON EARTH POSSESSED YOU?

When the disciples . . . saw this they said, "Lord, may we call down fire from heaven to burn them up?" But he turned and rebuked them. "You do not know," he said, "to what spirit you belong; for the Son of Man did not come to destroy men's lives but to save them."

Luke 9:54-56

Jesus' disciples are undoubtedly frustrated that the Samaritans are not welcoming their Lord and his message with open arms. Like many in every age who have something new to share, they think that what these dumb foreigners need is a little dose of force to change their hearts and minds. You can almost hear them muttering, "How dare these guys resist the good news we're bringing them. We'll fix them!"

So they go to Jesus and ask for authorization to call in fire on the enemy position. Notice how quickly the objects of their missionary zeal have become the "enemy." Imagine their surprise when their leader not only refuses to requisition fire from heaven but even questions just whose side they are on. "You do not know," he says, "to what spirit you belong; for the Son of Man did not come to destroy men's lives but to save them."

Jesus is not simply questioning their tactics. He is asking them what kind of spirit is leading them. As we might say, *"What on earth possessed you even to ask such a thing?"*

That is the issue in this story. It is also the issue in Paul's letter to the Galatians, where Paul says, "If the Spirit is the source of our life, let the Spirit also direct our course." It is a constant issue for us today: as individuals, as a church, as a nation.

I

What kind of spirit is leading us? It is not an easy question to answer, for we all have ways of giving different and sometimes deceptive names to the spirits that move us. We like to think that our inclination to make more money is motivated by a spirit of concern for our family's security. Someone looking at us from a less affluent corner of the world might just call it "greed." The settlers of the New World would probably have said that their westward expansion was led by a spirit of "adventure," or by something mysterious called "manifest destiny." The Native Americans who happened to be in their path might have called it by a different name, like "conquest." (The Spanish who occupied the American West built what they called "missions," but history calls their armies "conquistadores.")

Crusaders of any time like to say that they are apostles of some new and good thing: a new vision, a new order, a new freedom. Those whose land they occupy often find it hard to appreciate these wonders when they are offered at the point of a gun, so that what the newcomers call democracy may look to those who are being converted more like domination.

The disciples certainly felt that they were doing the Lord's work, spreading the news of God's Messiah. They could even feel that those who resisted them were resisting God and therefore deserved some kind of divine spanking. This is frequently true among religious folk. If we are spreading God's word as we understand it, we are tempted to be more than a little condescending toward those who understand God's word differently. So a bishop may feel entitled to deny communion to someone who does not agree with all his church's teachings. So church leaders may insist on reserving ordination for those who look and act like themselves. Such church leaders are certainly sincere in promoting what they believe are the central values of their faith. Yet it is fair to ask whether those in power are being led by a spirit that is too much defined by their own rules and institutions and interests.

II

And Jesus says, "You do not know to what spirit you belong." How do we know that we are being led by the Spirit of Christ and not some other spirit? How do we keep from deceiving ourselves with our rationalizations? Let me suggest three tests.

First, test the spirit. Check it out with others. Not just others of your own church or party or nation but others who really are *other,* who see the world through lenses unlike your own. Being a lone ranger may be heroic, but it can also be a convenient way to avoid negative feedback. A leader who doesn't listen to contrary opinions may be demonstrating the power of his convictions or he may simply not want anyone to confuse him with facts that don't fit into his plans.

Second, test yourself. Ask yourself as honestly and as carefully as you can just whose interests are being served, to what spirit do you belong, what on earth is "possessing" you in this moment? Ask yourself some hard questions: Am I seeking justice or just revenge? Democracy or domination? Purity of the faith or just conformity? Look in the mirror and try to answer these questions with a straight face.

Dig a little deeper. Pay attention to that side of yourself

– and your church and your culture and your nation – that we might call the "shadow side." Be aware that within each of us there are spirits that are constantly seeking to have their way, spirits with names like pride and anger and power and self-interest. Be aware that on this earth there is no pure soul, not even yours; no pure church, not even this one; no pure nation, not even our own.

It is not pessimistic or disloyal or unpatriotic to say this. It is simply an important truth to remember that may help us avoid the terribly self-deceiving fantasy that God's purposes and ours are always the same. Paul and Jesus were both quite realistic about that shadow side. Paul wrote about the constant war within himself. Jesus, in his matter-of-fact way, spoke of "you, who are evil, who know how to give good gifts to your children." Evil! He calls us evil! Jesus knows that human life is a constant struggle to be possessed by God's Spirit and not by those other spirits within us.

Reinhold Niebuhr was known as a Christian Realist. He insisted that we need to create and abide by laws because we are not good enough to do freely and consistently what needs to be done; we need to pay taxes because we cannot afford to leave the well being of our neighbors to the mercy of our good intentions and our occasional bursts of generosity; we need agreement among nations about standards of behavior (like the Geneva Conventions) because nations, like individuals, can rationalize brutal behavior when it fits their own interests or serves some lesser spirit that has taken hold of them.

Test the spirits. Test yourself. *Finally, make the Spirit of Christ your gold standard.* "You do not know," he said, "to what spirit you belong. For the Son of Man came not to destroy men's lives but to save them." Not to destroy but to save. That, it seems to me, is a good way to measure my motives and my actions. Do the choices I make seem likely to destroy or to heal, to build up or to tear down, to belittle or to nurture, to bring people together or to drive them apart? Are we as a church or a nation more interested in blaming others whose ways differ from ours than in finding common ground? Do our actions look more like domination than democracy?

Jesus showed us a different way, a different Spirit. He refused to give in to the spirit of anger of his disciples. Even more, he challenged them to face up to the spirits that possessed them, spirits of revenge, domination, destruction. He reminded them, and he reminds us, that he came not to destroy but to heal. God help us to be healed of the spirit of anger and self-righteousness and pride. God help us to be open to the Spirit of Christ in our hearts.

BELIEVING IS SEEING

*Earth's crammed with heaven,
And every common bush afire with God;
But only he who sees takes off his shoes,
The rest sit round it and pluck blackberries.
-Elizabeth Barrett Browning*

*Be Thou my Vision, O Lord of my heart;
Nought be all else to me save that Thou art—
Thou my best thought, by day or by night,
Waking or sleeping, Thy presence my light.
-Ancient Irish*

I DON'T WANT TO BE SCARED ANYMORE

There is no fear in love, but perfect love casts out fear.
I John 4:18

Most sermons start with the bad stuff. Like an insurance salesman warning of sudden disaster or a journalist writing a catchy lead, preachers usually begin with a problem: a question looking for an answer, a sinner looking for forgiveness, a lost traveler looking for a map, a sick soul looking for a cure.

Certainly that is usually the way I start. My wife, who has survived forty years of my sermons, can tell you that. An astute friend took note of it after only a year of exposure. That is the way I think. It is, certainly, the way I work as a counselor. I listen for the problem, the pain, the puzzle, and then I try to move toward a new or better possibility.

But it occurs to me that sometimes starting with the problem is the problem. Starting with our questions, our lostness, our sin or disease sets our minds on the wrong path to begin with. It occurs to me that starting our day by thinking of the problems we face may in fact put us in a frame of mind that colors everything we see and every decision we make.

So today I am going to break a lifelong tradition and start with the answer instead of the question, the good news instead of the bad. And you all have to promise to keep reading until I get to the bad stuff.

Here is the good news, the answer, the word of the

day: *There is no fear in love, for perfect love casts out fear.* He who fears, says John, has not had the love of God completed in him, for God is love. That is why the answer has to come first. Because God, the God who is love, comes first. Before our questions, before our wanderings and wonderings, before our struggles. Just as your love for your child came first, before the pangs of birth, the demands of childhood, the struggles of adolescence. Just as the Bible begins with Creation, which is itself an act of God's love. In his sermon called *Creation* James Weldon Johnson says it this way: "*Then God said, 'I'm lonely. I'll make me a world.*" God's act of creation is an act of love, just as your acts of creation – a song, a drawing, a meal, a garden, a child, a friendship – just as these are acts of love.

Knowing this makes a difference. Knowing that God is love before you begin to search for answers or maps or healing or comfort does something for your attitude. It is like knowing before you begin a difficult and dangerous voyage that the ocean is your home. That can make a difference. Let me try to show you what I mean.

Some people step out of their homes every morning into a world that seems more like a jungle than a garden, more a desert than a home. They start each day down a path that looks more like an obstacle course than a highway.

Some people walk into a room full of people and see competitors rather than companions, aliens rather than neighbors, possible enemies instead of potential friends.

Some people approach God in prayer like felons crouching before a judge who is eager to pass sentence, or shy children pleading with a demanding parent. Many more think of prayer as sending searching messages in the general direction of a vague, god-shaped hole in an empty sky.

What about you? How does the world look to you in the morning? Does it seem to be full of peril or opportunity? Is it a place of threat or of adventure? What do you see when you look at others? Are they mouths to feed, customers to please, managers to placate, drivers to resent, bores to avoid? Or are they simply faceless mannikins to ignore? And what about God? Is God a scowling boss, a sleepy grandparent, a relentlessly indifferent force, a benevolent blur?

How you look at the world, at people, at God – what lens you have in your spectacles – determines to a large extent whether you begin your day in fear or in confidence. In the hit movie *The Sixth Sense*, the psychologist asks Cole what he wants. Cole answers, "I can tell you what I don't want. I don't want to be scared anymore." That puts it in a nutshell for most of us, I think. *I don't want to be scared anymore.*

The writer of today's lesson says, "Fear has to do with punishment." I had a lot of trouble with that. It seems to me that fear has to do with a lot of things besides punishment. Then I realized that punishment comes in many forms. For you the greatest punishment may be rejection, poverty, failure. For someone else punishment may look like illness, death, abandonment. What we consider punishment is what we fear the most.

But what if we started the day with the answer instead of the question? What if we opened our doors into a world with all its dangers knowing that we were accompanied by the God who is love instead of feeling alone with all the things by which life can punish us? Make no mistake. Life can cause us much pain. The writer says, "perfect love casts out fear." He does not say that perfect love casts out pain.

There is plenty of pain in the world – from illness, from accident, from the violence that others do to us by word or action, by exploitation or neglect. There is pain that we inflict on ourselves by our own fears, like the child terrified of his own shadow. We cause ourselves pain by projecting our own worst thoughts and feelings onto others, then cringing to think that they will judge us as harshly as we judge ourselves.

There is the pain of living, the pain of losing, the pain of loving. Living causes pain, for things do not always go our way; accidents happen; failure is eventually a part of life for all of us. Losing causes pain, and all of us know something about loss. Even if you have not yet suffered the loss of someone close to you, you have surely suffered the loss of a dream, the loss of a pet, the loss of friends who move away, the progressive loss of physical abilities as the years pass. All of us know about the pain of loss. And loving causes pain. We take on pain when we choose to care about people. We can be hurt by their anger or rejection. And we can hurt for them and with them when they hurt (that is what compassion means). The only way to avoid the pain of loving is to shut ourselves away and keep anyone from getting close. And then we have to deal with the pain of loneliness and unlived life.

Being surrounded by the love of God does not protect us from pain but from the fear of what that pain can do to us. Knowing that we are embraced in the love of the God in whom we live and move and have our being means that pain can hurt us but not destroy us. It means that nothing that living or losing or loving can do to us can separate us from that loving God.

In the gospel lesson Jesus says, "I am the vine, you are the branches; abide in my love." What does it mean to abide in the vine? It means "make yourself at home, settle in, put down your roots in the vine that is God."

Here is another way to think of it. Think of yourself as a wave on an ocean. You and I, each of us, are waves on the water, and the water is God. We are all knocked about by the winds that stir the water, and sometimes we even feel threatened by other waves, because they seem bigger or stronger or angrier than we. Some of the winds – or spirits, the word is the same – seem to be winds of strife that turn waves against each other and make us afraid.

Then remember. Remember that nothing can separate a wave from the water – or from other waves, for that matter. Remember that along with the spirits of strife that stir up the waves there is another spirit, another creative wind, that moves over the water. And that wind is also God. So God is the water and God is the wind, and both the water and the wind embrace us and move us with love.

When the disciples found themselves on a stormy sea they were afraid. Then they remembered that on the boat with them was one whom "even the winds and the sea obeyed." They still had to navigate in their little boat. But they discovered a presence that took away their fear.

We still have to navigate on what sometimes will be a very stormy sea. We can still be hurt by the accidents of living and losing, and by the choices of loving. But it makes a difference to start with the answer instead of the fearful question. Before you open the door each day into a world full of problems and puzzles and people who may or may not treat you well, remember the answer that can take away much of your fear. Remember that you abide in God, and that God is love.

THE WITCHES OF FORT LAUDERDALE

I was probably not terribly different from most kids. My everyday childhood world was inhabited by a colorful and sometimes scary cast of characters: heroes, parents, schoolteachers, tooth fairies, relatives, phantoms, playmates, lone rangers, godmothers, ape men, talking ducks, and witches. Especially witches. I heard stories of children in the woods who found their way to gingerbread houses. I heard of magic charms that could put children to sleep forever. My earliest movie memories from those pre-TV days were Snow White and The Wizard of Oz, and the characters that left the deepest imprint on my fertile imagination were those scary women who threatened Snow White and Dorothy and even Toto.

It shouldn't be surprising then that one of the most vivid and memorable encounters from that time should have certain supernatural overtones. It happened on an ordinary day, close to Christmas I believe, on an ordinary walk down Broward Boulevard in Fort Lauderdale. My favorite aunt, whom we called Ibbie, was walking with me and my big brother Danny. We were about six and four years old, Danny and I, and he had, if anything, a more active and sinister fantasy life than I.

As we approached what I now know was a large Roman Catholic church, two black robed nuns emerged from a side door, entered the sidewalk and turned toward us. "Witches!" yelled Danny. "Ghosts!" echoed little brother. Danny turned and fled toward home, followed closely by his small and loyal shadow. Ibbie pursued a little further back, laughing and calling after us, trying in vain to stop our panicky retreat and calm our pounding hearts.

My encounter with the witches of Fort Lauderdale is one of the most vivid of my early memories. It is not, fortunately for my mental health, the most powerful, lasting or deeply felt. The presence of that loving aunt provided a strong counterbalance of grace to what would, without her, have been much more traumatic than it was. I can remember Danny's wild dash toward home and my fearful pursuit. But I can also remember Ibbie's laughter and her reassuring presence.

Ibbie spent many Christmases with us over the years, as did my beloved Uncle Dave. Their generosity and gentleness, along with that of my parents, somehow embodied the most important message that the story of Christmas had to tell. The impact of their lives left me with a confidence that no matter what witches and other dangerous spirits might inhabit my world – or even my own small self – they were not the most powerful or the most important spirits at work.

If there were witches, there were also angels. If there was fear, there was also "Fear not." If evil had a place in the world, so did the love which came and comes into our life at Christmas. Later on, when I discovered Shakespeare, I could know what he meant when, speaking of the season of Christ's birth, he wrote, "no fairy strikes, nor witch hath power to charm; so hallowed and so gracious is the time."

THE HINGE OF HISTORY

Two men, moved by the Spirit, speak to people of their own time and to us. One man, the prophet known as Jeremiah, writes to a people far from home, hungry for some word that God has not forgotten them in their captivity. The second man, the evangelist we call John, writes to a people whose very homeland is possessed by the Roman conqueror. Both people, hundreds of years apart, live in a world darkened by tyranny and by the bitterness and despair of their own hearts.

Listen now for a word from God to us, first in the words of Jeremiah:

'Thus says the Lord: Keep your voice from weeping and your eyes from tears; for there is reward for your work, says the Lord. They shall come back from the land of the enemy; there is hope for your future, says the Lord.

The days are surely coming, says the Lord, when I will make a new covenant with the house of Israel . . . I will put my law within them, and I will write it on their hearts; and I will be their God, and they shall be my people."

And then these words from John:

In the beginning was the Word, and the Word was with God, and the Word was God. He was in the beginning with God. All things came through him, and without him not one thing came into being. What has come into being in him was life, and the life was the light of all people. The light is shining in the darkness, and the darkness has not overcome it."

What is the difference between the word of Jeremiah and the word of John? Why do they both speak to us with such power? What can it mean to us to believe with all our being that John's word, not Jeremiah's, is indeed the last word?

I

What is the difference between these two powerful words? *Simply this. Jeremiah's word is a word of hope. John's word is a word of history.* No one has spoken hope more eloquently than the prophet to the exiles. No one has held out for a people in darkness a better vision of the future. Jeremiah's word is supremely a word of hope to a people who still live in an age when God seems mostly absent. And no one has more clearly or succinctly stated the new thing that has happened than does John in the simple and profound words with which he begins to tell of the Christ. No one has named more dramatically the new fact of history which has caused us to rewrite our calendars even though it has not completely rewritten our lives.

Jeremiah speaks of what God will do. John writes of what God has done. Jeremiah's is a word of expectation; John's is a word of fulfillment. We live in 1999 A.D. - anno domini. "The Year of our Lord". So why is it that Jeremiah's words speak to us with as much power as John's. Why is it that after two thousand years we still respond to such a word of hope?

Perhaps it is because a part of us is still living where Jeremiah lived - before Christ. Perhaps in our hearts we are all a little bit – or a lot – BC men and women. We still wait for God as though he were absent. We long for a word from God as though that Word had not become flesh. We live in a state of darkness as though the dawn had not come.

In many ways ours is still a BC world. We have known Christ's way of living among us for two thousand years, yet still argue about theology and morals as though Jeremiah's promise of a law written in our hearts were still a long way off In our BC world security and diversion are more important than love and sacrifice, just as though Christ had not come. In our BC world men and women spend too much money on cars to make him feel powerful and clothes to make her feel beautiful, as though enough power or enough beauty would fill their empty BC hearts. In our BC world a young woman hopes to make $20 thousand a year working with disturbed children; a young man makes ten times that amount helping people manipulate their financial holdings; another young man is guaranteed ten times that amount for throwing a round ball through a hoop and allowing people to use his name to sell shoes many children cannot afford.

The BC man or woman within us lives in fear- as though God were absent. He tries to earn a place for himself - as though God had not already done that for him. She worries that she will not be accepted by those whose regard she thinks she needs - as though her acceptance were not already a given. Jeremiah's words speak to us because they speak to our BC hearts. And as long as we live as though Christ had not already come, we will continue to long for what Jeremiah promises.

What could it mean for us to believe with all our being that John's word - not Jeremiah's – is truly the last word? Let me suggest two things.

II

First, it would mean living life in the presence of God rather than in God's absence. Before the coming of the

Christ, people had only glimpses of God or words from godly men and women who told them that God was near. Even those whose walk with God was the closest had only their hope and their faith to sustain them.

To live life in the presence of God rather than his absence is to know that God is not absent but merely hidden. Someone has suggested that *hiddenness is a necessary part of God's relationship to us.* God is hidden as an anchor is hidden if it is to secure a ship, as the air we breathe is hidden if it is to sustain us without clouding our vision, as the source of light is hidden in a painting by Rembrandt. God is hidden from us in order to sustain us, to inspire us, to illuminate our lives. But God is not absent. Not if we truly trust that John's word is the last word.

Second, it would mean living our lives in the confidence that the rule of God in the world has already begun, even though much of the time the sphere of that rule seems terribly limited in our own lives or in the life of our society. John says that the light has already come into the world and that the world in its darkness has not overcome it. Another translation has it, "the darkness comprehended it not". Well that's true too. We don't understand it. We cannot overcome it. We can only believe that the light has come.

Tennessee Williams' powerful play *The Glass Menagerie* ends when Tom leaves the home of his mother and his crippled sister Laura after another moment of hope for Laura has, as her mother Amanda puts it, "turned out badly". Over the miles Tom speaks to his sister, for although he has left her he cannot banish her from his memory or his heart. "Nowadays", Tom says, "the world is lit by lightning".

What does it mean to live in a world "lit by lightning"? Let me describe it through the eyes of a child. One of my earliest memories is that of trying to go to sleep in a darkened bedroom. My brother, fast asleep, could not keep me company. My parents had closed the door so that lights and noises would not keep me awake. On stormy nights when the world outside was lit by lightning, I can remember the glimpses I had of my room. Some of the glimpses were reassuring - familiar furniture and the favorite teddy bear on the bed beside me. Other glimpses were scary. Was that long thing by the window really just a robe hanging on a hook? Or was it something else? Sometimes the darkness between the lightning flashes gave me time to put my most fearful imaginings to work.

To those BC persons in the days of Jeremiah, as well as to all of us BC men and women in the day of Tennessee Williams, the world is lit by lightning. Some of the lightning is that of human wisdom and human love, which gives us glimpses of a better world. Some other lightning is the lightning of human hatred and violence, which creates frightening shadows and makes us unsure of our future. And sometimes, between the lightning flashes, we may feel overwhelmed by the darkness that we know is out there- the darkness of war, of poverty, of human indifference, of willful exploitation of the weak; as well as the darkness that is in here, the intractable, stubborn darkness in our own hearts.

For the child in that dark room the most welcome ray of light was that which came when one of my parents responded to my pleas and "opened the door just a crack". The narrow column of light that split the dark room was not enough to see much. But it was enough to help me feel in touch with those other rooms where my parents were awake. It was enough to remind me of that world of light beyond my own small dark room.

Someone has spoken of Christ as the "hinge of history". What they mean, of course, is that Christ is the one about whom time itself now pivots – so that all of history is "before Christ" or "in the year of our Lord". Remembering that frightened child in that dark room, I like to think that Christ is the hinge of history in another sense. I like to think that Christ is that door, opened just a crack, through whom the light of God sends a single constant beam into our dark world.

The darkness to which John spoke is real, like the darkness to which Jeremiah spoke, or Tennessee Williams. But to peer into that darkness with a BC heart is to forget, or at least fail to trust, that the hinge of history called the Christ has opened a crack in the door to give us a glimpse of that eternal world that could and can and will flood our dark world with light as surely as we open our BC hearts and churches and cities and allow it to come in.

A TURNING POINT

When I think of turning points I think of the Union Seminary library on a spring day of my senior year. I had already begun to think about freezing my Deep South bones in Aberdeen on the north coast of Scotland, where I had corresponded with Archibald Hunter about pursuing a PhD in Biblical Studies. I was convinced that I was on my way to frostbite and a doctorate and maybe even a Scottish accent.

In the library I found myself thumbing through catalogues of other seminaries and divinity schools. I don't know why. Habit perhaps, or maybe I was hoping to find – or be found by – something. I picked up the catalogue of Harvard Divinity School, a place somewhat suspect in my then neo-orthodox mind. My eye fell upon a course title that turned my life in a new direction. "Theological Anthropology" was the title, Hans Hoffman the professor. I cannot quote any of the course description, but I can remember my excitement. For some reason I knew that I had to find out more. I read more about the school and about Hans Hoffman. I discovered that he was Swiss, that he had studied with Karl Barth, attended the Jung Institute, written about Reinhold Niebuhr. I arranged to meet him, visited Cambridge, wrote a polite letter to Archibald Hunter to terminate a relationship that had never begun.

That spring day in the library turned my life in a new direction. I began, as I explained it to myself at the time, to focus on the human end of the divine human encounter. I wanted to know more about the people who needed to hear the gospel rather than the documents that proclaimed it. I *felt reasonably clear (rightly or wrongly) from my seminary days what the message was. I was not so clear about the puzzling creatures (among whom I numbered myself) who needed to hear the message.*

So I went to Harvard, where I spent a cold winter discovering the world outside the southern Presbyterian Church. I discovered Christians who were not Presbyterian, not even Protestant. I found my year in Cambridge exciting, threatening, lonely, confusing. I talked to Hans Hoffman, a lively and encouraging young teacher who kept telling his students to pay attention to "what the Holy Spirit is doing these days." I also talked about my own personal confusion and growing depression. He was the first teacher who ever encouraged me to take time off to get my head straight rather than plow ahead on an academic track. I was grateful, and I took his advice.

He gave me the name of a therapist in Washington D.C., a German expatriate named Hanna Colm, a friend of Paul Tillich. In order to work with her, I found a church job nearby in Maryland. My three years in Towson gave me the opportunity to meet two important women: Hanna my therapist and Lynn my future wife. Those years also introduced me to church members who owned a schoolhouse in Vermont that eventually became our own summer second home. Years later our oldest daughter met her husband there. I sometimes think back to that catalogue in the seminary library which led me to a series of discoveries – of myself, my wife, my daughters, and my grandchildren. I believe that I learned, as my professor would put it, "what the Holy Spirit is doing these days."

ONLY THOSE WHO SEE

When all things began, the Word was at the creation. The Word dwelt with God, and what God was, the Word was. The Word, then, was with God at the beginning, and through the Word all things came to be: no single thing came into being without him. All that came to be was alive with his life, and that life was the light of humankind. The light shines on in the dark, and the darkness has never mastered it.

John 1:1-5

I went with my daughter Kate to help water the tigers at the wildlife preserve. I did some useful things like hooking up and unhooking the hoses, and some daring things like petting the baby white tiger in the farmhouse. Most of the time, though, I simply watched and wondered. I wondered at Kate, who talked to those huge fearsome creatures as though they were her little brothers and sisters (which she clearly believes they are). I wondered about the fifteen foot chain link fence and fervently hoped that it was strong enough to contain her eight hundred pound siblings. I wondered at the incredible union of power and grace and beauty that moved back and forth before my eyes. Once again I knew that I was getting a glimpse of God's creative Spirit at work.

From the very beginning, says the writer of today's gospel, God has been speaking. It is a part of the nature of God to speak. Indeed everything that comes into being is a part of the divine self-expression. God's creative word takes shape in the world of nature, and we give it names like tiger and sequoia, penguin and violet. God's self-expression shines through human beings who seem to be touched by Spirit as instruments. We call that touch inspiration, and those who seem to be vehicles of the Divine we call prophets, or artists, or saints.

The creative word of God is always speaking. We may say that God speaks in the word of the psalmist, in the music of Beethoven, in the art of Georgia O'Keefe, the leadership of Gandhi, the fingers of Horowitz, the voice of Maya Angelou, the poetry of Shakespeare. But is God's self revelation only to be glimpsed in the tigers of the natural order and in those flashes of lightning we call human genius?

Not at all. The very point of John's most profound of introductions is that God's Word has been constantly speaking through everything that comes into being, that God has in fact become embodied in the very midst of life. And that we tend to look right over it. "The light shines in the darkness," says John, "and the darkness has not mastered it." Other translations say "comprehended it not" or "understood it not." A few lines further on John repeats, "He came into his own home, and his own people did not recognize him."

A boy and his father talk about prayer. The father asks his son what he prays about. "Always the same thing," the boy replies. "I'm always praying for God to show me that He is real." So are we all, all constantly praying for God to show us that He or She is real, and at the same time constantly missing the self-revealing of God that is present in our very midst.

Well, if God is constantly being revealed, where should we be looking? Let me suggest three places.

We tend to look for God in the spectacular. We should be looking as much in the commonplace.

It is hard not to sense something of God's presence in

the Tiger. It is easy to remember moments of deliverance as evidence that God is at work in the world. All of us remember moments when we heard something of the divine at work as we listened to a choir sing *Messiah* or a pianist play Chopin.

But John reminds us that God is present in every moment of creation. Not just in the grandeur of human invention and the spectacular touches of creation, but even more in the daily epiphanies of God's presence – in the intricacies of the tiniest flower, the everyday miracle of birth, the constant beauty of the night sky. Elizabeth Barrett Browning puts it this way: *Earth's crammed with heaven, And every common bush afire with God; But only he who sees, takes off his shoes, The rest sit round it and pluck blackberries . . .*

We tend to look for God in demonstrations of power. But we should be looking as much in moments of gentleness.

It is easy to be impressed by the power of the Hurricane and by the "lifestyle of the rich and famous." It is easy to allow ourselves to be captivated by the staterooms of the Titanic, the mansion of Bill Gates, the gowns of Princess Diana. So it is all the more important to be reminded, as Elijah was reminded on the mountain of God, that God's voice spoke most clearly in the silence that followed the earthquake, wind and fire. It is all the more important to remember that angel voices and bright stars were only pointers to the real epiphany of God which happened in a silent, tiny stable.

People over the centuries have wrestled with this question. Why would God elect to appear in a child born out of wedlock to a blue collar family on a side road of civilization?

Perhaps because that is the way God's self-revelation happens best: in ways that do not overpower us; ways that invite us to discover God's presence in our own lives. If God were only revealed in Hurricanes and Emperors, we might be intimidated into giving God our respect, but we could hardly make a free choice to respond in love. If God appeared only in the lives of Presidents or CEO's or Admirals, we would probably watch the momentous event on the Evening News and then go back to our ordinary lives feeling more marginal than ever.

The truly startling news of John's Gospel is this, that the culmination of God's self-revealing incarnation took place in the child of a refugee family living in a trailer park.

We tend to look for God in the past. We should be looking just as much in the present.

When the Hebrews fled from Egypt, they had to be reminded constantly that God went before them into the wilderness. It was much easier to think of God as dwelling in the traditions of the past. And Christians living at the end of a millennium may find themselves longing for the comforting securities of a time when nobody asked questions and everyone knew his place.

Because we tend to identify the revelation of God as something that happened in a particular time and place, we are tempted to think that somehow that time and that place are different from our own –that that place is "holier" than our own, that time closer to God than our time. So we must remind ourselves that while the Age of Caesar may be the Age of the Christ, so the last two millennia, including our own century, could be called the Age of the Spirit.

How will people remember the twentieth century? Will it be the century of air travel? The century of the computer? Maybe it will be remembered primarily as a century of war and of holocaust on a scale never before known. Maybe. Or maybe people will look back and say that our time saw an explosion of liberating spiritual power that had not been seen since the century of the Christ.

People in every age have been led by the Spirit to do new things, open new doors. And other people in those same times, people who felt that God had already done his thing in an earlier time, those people have tried to close those doors.

George Bernard Shaw wrote a play called *Saint Joan,* relating the story of the French peasant girl who felt called of God to lead her people into battle. At the end of the play the God-intoxicated young woman is sent to the fire by the rulers of church and state who are frightened by her visions and her potential for upsetting the established order. In the epilogue, one of the observers asks this sad, disturbing question: *Must then a Christ perish in torment in every age to save those that have no imagination?* That is a question that should disturb our sleep a bit. Must a Christ perish in torment in our age because we have no imagination?

Can you find within yourself the spiritual imagination to see God's creative presence in the everyday miracles of life? Can I discover within myself the compassionate imagination to discern the Image of God hidden beneath the blemishes and scars of my fellow human beings? Even those – especially those – whose ways offend me, whose accents turn me off, whose pain escapes my notice? And what of those who struggle for acceptance and dignity – those minorities and outsiders, those dispossessed and eccentrics, those shepherds and lepers of our time. Can we find within ourselves the moral imagination to see in their struggles the movement of God's liberating Spirit in our own time?

The Word of God made flesh is more than an explanation to tell us about who God was and what God did in some other time and some other place. It is an encounter that can awaken our imagination and open our eyes. The Word of God made flesh is more than communication about God, it is communion with God – the God who is always and everywhere present; in the tiger and the lamb, in this place and in the place where you work, in those whom you love and those whom you despise. *Earth's crammed with heaven, and every common bush afire with God. But only those who see take off their shoes.* May God help me, may God help you to be one of those who see.

UNDISCOVERED COUNTRY

For with that sleep of death, what dreams may come when we have shuffled off this mortal coil must give us pause...

It is no accident that Hamlet has been a figure of such fascination to actors, readers and theatergoers for centuries. No accident, either, that his most famous words, memorized by generations of students, have such compelling force.

To be or not to be. Hamlet speaks of the elemental choice of life or death and of the painful forces that tug us one way and then the other. But it is not only potential suicides for whom he speaks when he realizes exactly why he holds on, however reluctantly, to life.

Who would fardels bear, he asks, *to grunt and sweat under a weary life, but that the dread of something after death, the undiscovered country from whose bourn no traveler returns, puzzles the will, and makes us rather bear those ills we have than fly to others that we know not of?*

What is that "something after death," that "undiscovered country" which strikes such dread? Hamlet, we suppose, is thinking of a life after physical death. But what about the death of a favorite dream? What of the loss of a desperately needed habit? What of the death of a treasured relationship to which I cling even when I can taste its poison? What of the dread I feel when I try to imagine life beyond deaths such as these?

Physical death is not the only passageway to undiscovered country. Life itself seems to be a constant procession of deaths, and we find ourselves faced again and again with "the dread of something after death." "How will

I get along," I ask myself, "if I leave the person who has made a secure nest for me?" "What will happen to me if I give up the addiction that has comforted me for so long?" "What will life be like if I let go the familiar, repulsive, beloved, stifling image of myself that I have held since childhood?"

Think of the pilgrimage we call psychotherapy as a journey through a series of deaths, a journey in which we must face again and again our dread of undiscovered country. Those of us who have been on the journey and those of us who accompany others know how frightening it is to enter that passage or to open some of the doors along the way. Changing our relationships or our lifestyle or our inner landscape means facing death: death of the familiar, death of the tried and true, death of the fables we tell ourselves to comfort ourselves. And no one, we all know, wants to let go the lifebuoy to which he clings until he sees a boat on the horizon.

Because this is true, the greatest need for those at the brink, or in the middle, of psychotherapy is the need for hope – hope that we will survive the changes we face, hope that life will be better on the other side of change, hope that there is indeed life after the particular death we are facing.

As a therapist I may lend some of my own hope until the one on the journey discovers some for himself. "Yes," I may say, "I believe that you can make it. Yes, I am confident that you will find your own undiscovered country worth the journey." As a pastoral counselor I may bear witness to my belief and experience that new life can and does come precisely through and as a result of death. Unless and until the seed dies, it cannot produce the new plant.

My faith in resurrection has to do with more than an ancient drama played out in a rocky Middle Eastern garden, more, even, than a personal confidence that somehow, beyond understanding, that drama offers me the promise of new life beyond the grave. Faith in resurrection means something for me as a human being who must in my own lifetime face many deaths and explore much undiscovered country. It means that I can open the doors of that journey with some reason to hope that there will be a new and even better place on the other side of my "necessary losses."

For me, as a counselor, such a faith enables me to say to my hesitant, courageous, wary, venturesome fellow pilgrim, "Open the door when you are ready. The passageway will be dark, but in the undiscovered country you will find yourself in ways you never imagined."

TWO PART INVENTION

...we observed his star in its rising and have come to pay him homage.
Matthew 2:2

...the true light, which enlightens everyone, was coming into the world... yet the world did not know him.
John 1:9-10

The families who invited me to help organize a new Presbyterian church in rural northern Virginia had bought a tiny church building that had been vacated by the Episcopalians. The building consisted of a sanctuary that seated one hundred – if they were very friendly – and a one room basement that served as a nursery. That was it. Connecting the two floors was a very narrow wooden spiral staircase, the door of which opened right beside the pulpit.
    From time to time the quiet period before worship was jarred by a loud thunk, an unhappy sound that told us that someone climbing the staircase had bumped his or her poor head on the wooden beam near the top of the flight. There were, I am sure, some passionate silent prayers offered in that staircase concerning that beam (and maybe even concerning the Episcopalians who built it). But we in the sanctuary heard only the thunk.
    Well, I decided to look for some theologically appropriate way to warn unsuspecting climbers and at the same time prepare them for worship. In a religious bookstore I came upon the perfect solution, a beautiful

poster with an inspiring and cautionary message which I taped in the stairwell just beneath the offending beam. The message went like this: "If you do not raise your eyes you will think you are at the highest point."

On Epiphany we remember the three magi, and how they came over the centuries to be known as wise men. They were, first of all, willing to raise their eyes. That, it seems to me, is the first rule for anyone who is hoping to experience an epiphany. If you do not raise your eyes you will think you are at the highest point. In some situations you may bump your head. In every situation you will certainly miss whatever lies above or beyond your narrow range of vision.

Epiphany. We have come to associate the word with a special day of the church year. January 6th to be exact, the day after the 12th Day of Christmas, (twelve drummers drumming and all). But epiphany is not something for magi only. Epiphany is a wonderful constant possibility for any of us. And it begins when we raise our eyes.

Epiphany. The dictionary puts it this way: "an intuitive perception of, or insight into, the reality or essential meaning of something, usually initiated by some commonplace occurrence". Three men saw a star and said, "God has a message for humankind." One man met a peasant teacher and said, "The Divine Word has become flesh and dwelt in our midst." Here is a shorter definition: an epiphany is when the light bulb comes on and we say, "Oh, I get it! Yes. Yes!"

An epiphany is not a vision or a voice. You don't have to be a saint or a mystic, a prophet or a druggie to have one. An epiphany can happen for anyone. You might call it a "two part invention", part divine revelation and part human realization. For an epiphany you have to have both. For example, the magi could have looked through their first century telescopes and said, "Oh look, another star. That makes 1,975." No epiphany. To see a star and to realize that there is a message in the star, that is epiphany.

So, what part do we play in making ourselves open to our own epiphany? Or, to put it another way, what can the magi teach us that will make us wise? Let me suggest three things we can learn from the magi (one, of course, for each wise man).

I

First, we have to be willing to raise our eyes. That is not as simple as it sounds. Many very smart people in our day (we might even call them wise men) find it very difficult to raise their eyes. Some modern scientific and technological magi seem to be trapped in the notion that reality extends only as far as the eye can see. Huston Smith calls it tunnel vision, a view of reality that is limited to what we know as the material world. Our whole modern worldview is built around this tunnel vision. The great achievements of science tempt us to buy into this vision without question.

But raising our eyes is the first step toward becoming wise. Raising our eyes means looking beyond what our telescopes and microscopes show us. In some cases it means looking beneath the surface, seeking out the depths of life rather than settling for the rather simple notion that only what is visible on the surface is real. I think we all know better. I think we all know the truth of what the fox says when he tells the little prince: "It is only with the heart that one can see rightly; what is essential is invisible to the eye."

Raising our eyes means looking for meaning and purpose beyond what we see. It means paying attention to the world of spirit that surrounds and even invades the world of things in which we are immersed. It means cleansing the lenses of our spectacles so that we are able to see more, to see with the eye of the soul. As William Blake put it, "If the doors of perception were cleansed, we would see everything as it is: infinite."

II

Second, we must be ready to pack our bags. The magi were wise enough to know that not all the answers are to be found in our own back yards. And they were courageous enough to pack their bags and follow wherever the star led them.

Again, this is not as easy as it sounds. It is not so much the traveling that scares us. Some of us like to travel to new places. Sometimes we even learn something new while we are there. More times we come back saying there's no place like home. Some years ago, when a young Greek exchange student was visiting us we took her to see the sights of Washington. It was a particularly bright, clear day, which inspired my wife to say, "Isn't the sky a beautiful blue today!" Our homesick young visitor replied, "It is always like this in Greece." It is not disdain for travel that gets in our way so much as loyalty—loyalty to the place and the people, the language and the culture in which we have been nurtured. Sometimes our loyalty to what is familiar becomes a barrier to discovering what is true.

This is especially so in matters of faith. We tend to be possessive about our faith tradition, so that it is hard for us to believe that those who see God through other lenses may have something to share with us. Packing our bags does not always mean taking a trip. It may mean simply packing up the mental and emotional baggage that keeps us from seeing or appreciating a sky that is a different shade of blue from our own. Both the magi and the gospel writer had the wisdom – and the courage – to follow beyond their own tradition the leading of God's star.

III

Finally, we must be prepared to wonder. Wondering means questioning. The magi were seekers, willing to ask questions, willing to travel, willing even to change their minds and their itinerary. Those who are wise know that we always have more questions than answers, that even many of our answers are provisional ones. Those who are wise know that under the weight of the deepest questions of life the language of our answers bends and sometimes breaks.

Wondering also means marveling. The magi came with gifts for the newborn king. If they were surprised to find him among peasants, they were willing to marvel at this new kind of kingship and still present their gifts. They were, apparently, enough in awe of God's ways in the world that they kept their sense of wonder even in such a strange, unroyal place.

And what about us? Can we wait for our epiphanies with a sense of wonder? Can we look at the commonplace with open, questioning minds? Even more, can we let the wonder of life strike us in such a way that every experience becomes a moment in which God's presence touches us? Can we, like William Blake, *see the world in a grain of sand and a heaven in a wild flower?* Can we understand as Blake did that *if the doors of perception were cleansed, everything would appear as it is, infinite.*

The magi saw a star and realized that something of God was being revealed. The gospel writer met a man and called him "the true light that enlightens everyone." And we, if we will raise our eyes, can allow God's Spirit to enlighten us, to speak to us in every star, every wild flower, every human being whose life touches ours. That is a good way, I think, to start a new year, with eyes and hearts and imagination open to the epiphanies that are waiting for us around every corner.

KING LEAR REVISITED

I first saw "King Lear" when I was twenty-eight years old and newly married. Two weeks earlier I had made the journey home to Georgia for my father's funeral. The tears I shed in the darkened theater in Stratford, Connecticut were the tears of a son witnessing again the deterioration and death of a father.

I next saw "King Lear" a few years ago in my own home, watching transfixed by Olivier's stunning television portrayal. Twenty years had passed. I, like King Lear, was father to three daughters. Again I wept in a darkened room, again moved deeply by the same story. But this time I wept with Lear, not for him. This time I was the father, struggling to let go his claim on his children even as he longed to keep some cherished place in their lives.

Two visits to the same place twenty years apart. I discovered why some stories are worth reading or watching more than once. Not because we were too dull to understand the first time, or too shallow, but because each time we are able to see into the story from a different vantage point. We need to revisit the story not because the story has changed but because we have.

Therapists change with the years for many reasons. They have learned what works and what does not; they have read more, listened more, thought more. But also because they, like the young man losing a father who had become a father losing his daughters, they enter their clients' stories through a different door. Not better, just different. When a middle-aged counselor meets with a family whose son is struggling to break away he will remember how the son felt. But he will also know how the parents are feeling in a way he could never have known before.

Partners in marriage change too. Sometimes their new perspectives make them doubt the wisdom or even the validity of their earlier perceptions and decisions – or those of their mate. "I didn't know her at all," he sighs. "He never really loved me," she complains. Wrong. He knew her as well as he was capable of knowing her and as much as she could let herself be known. And he did love her, as much as he was capable of loving the person he knew at that time. It is unfair to second guess the perceptions and commitments of our younger selves. To do so is to demand that one twenty-five year old see another twenty-five year old through the eyes of the forty-something he/she has become.

If you revisit "King Lear" or some other family drama closer to home, allow your experience to give you a new look, a new capacity for empathy, a new door into the story. Make the most of a vision enlarged and enriched by time. But never despise the vision of your own past self. Youth sees in imagination what experience sees in memory. Youth may therefore be more hopeful and more demanding; experience may be more realistic and more forgiving. Neither vision is wrong. Every reading of "King Lear" has its own value.

BEHIND THE VEIL

...a cloud came and overshadowed them; and they were terrified.

Luke 9:34

Someone has said that the Bible is the story of a conversation between two worlds, the world of Spirit and our Human world. Well, the account in Luke's gospel sounds more like an invasion than a conversation. William James once said that we are separated from the spiritual dimension by a thin veil of consciousness. Well, the disciples must have felt as though that veil had been snatched away.

The story of the Transfiguration is a dramatic, multimedia account of a mystical experience: there is a dazzling light, a pair of visitors from another sphere, a booming voice coming out of the clouds. No wonder the disciples were terrified. All kinds of associations come to mind. We remember the story of Moses and how his face shone when he had been with God on Sinai and how the people of Israel asked him to wear a veil; we hear of Moses and Elijah and wonder about the possibility of some kind of return; we read of the voice from the heavens and recall Jesus' baptism and how a divine voice identified Jesus in a special way.

How do we react to this dramatic, mysterious story? Like the children of Israel we may want to veil our faces, to say that such mystical stuff is more than we can handle. Or, like Peter, we may want to do the opposite, to capture the experience. Anyone who has ever had, however briefly, a glimpse behind that veil can understand Peter. People have erected holy places, set aside holy times in an effort to hold on to the moment.

But the story seems to me to point beyond itself. It is clear that Jesus and his disciples are not going to stay on the mountaintop, and neither can we. So I want to invite you to think with me about this mysterious story by asking three questions about these moments when the veil is pulled aside. What are they like? What are they for? Can we do anything to pull the veil aside ourselves?

I

First, what are they like? The story in Luke today included a light, a vision and a voice. But that is not necessarily what happens every time. This glimpsing of another reality seems to take many shapes. Let me share with you four brief accounts from a variety of sources: Two poets, one Irish and one Indian, an English clergyman, an American monk.

William Butler Yeats:

> *My fiftieth year had come and gone,*
> *I sat, a solitary man, in a crowded London shop,*
> *An open book and empty cup*
> *On the marble table top.*
> *While on the shop and street I gazed,*
> *My body of a sudden blazed;*
> *And twenty minutes more or less*
> *It seemed, so great my happiness*
> *That I was blessed and could bless.*

Rabindranath Tagore:

I suddenly felt as if some ancient mist had in a moment lifted from my sight and the ultimate significance of all things was laid bare . . . Immediately I found the world bathed in a wonderful radiance . . .and no person or thing in the world seemed to me trivial or unpleasing.

Leslie Weatherhead:

For a few seconds only, I suppose, the whole train compartment was filled with light. . . I felt caught up into some tremendous sense of being within a loving, triumphant and shining purpose . . . All men were glorious beings who in the end would enter incredible joy. . . In a few moments the glory departed – all but one curious, lingering feeling. I loved everybody in that compartment . . . at that moment I think I would have died for any one of the people in that compartment.

Thomas Merton:

Life is this simple. We are living in a world that is absolutely transparent, and God is shining through it all the time. This is not just a fable or a nice story. It is true . . .God shows himself everywhere, in everything – in people and in things and in nature and in events . . . God is everywhere and in everything and we cannot be without him. It's impossible. The only thing is that we don't see it.

I think that is enough to get the flavor. These momentary glimpses behind the veil are sudden, elusive, deeply compelling. They do not usually include voices or visions, but they do produce a profound sense of another reality, a new appreciation of the beauty of the world, a powerful wish to reach out to others. Yeats said it in one line: "I was blessed and could bless."

These descriptions may sound foreign to your experience, even a little weird. Yet they seem to be happening all the time to a lot of people, and those people are never quite the same. They certainly happened to the disciples, and so we need to wonder just what they mean.

II

What are they for? Well, it seems clear to me that they are not an end in themselves, but a *way of pointing us toward a different way of being in the world*. Each of the experiences we heard pointed toward a more positive attitude toward other people. The stories that follow the disciples' experience on the mountain seem to make the same point. Jesus is immediately called upon to heal a boy who is demon possessed. The disciples complain that others are healing in another name and Jesus says, "Let them be, healing is healing." In short, when the world of spirit enters the world of human pain, the life we are called to lead is a life whose attitude toward others is defined by compassion. Not dominance, not judgment, not indifference, but compassion.

Immediately after these events we are told that Jesus "set his face to go to Jerusalem," to a place where he would come into conflict with institutions of human power which used that power to dominate and exploit other human beings. And his awareness of the presence of spirit meant that he, and those who follow him, would bring to those institutions an attitude of confrontation. He would be saying to them, in effect, what you call the "powers that be" are not the power that was and is and shall be. Paul

Walking to Wisdom

Tillich has said that the difference between mystical religion and prophetic religion is just this: that in prophetic religion the setting aside of the veil leads us to go back into the world with a new way of being, with an attitude of compassion for those in pain and an attitude of confrontation with those in power.

We are not invited to use any mystical awareness of the spiritual reality behind the veil as a way of escaping everyday life but as a way of seeing all of life in a new light. Nothing in our valleys of pain, nothing in our Jerusalems of power is ever the same when, having had a glimpse behind the veil, we go back to everyday life knowing that God is present.

III

Final question. Can we do anything to pull the veil aside? The answer is no and yes. No, we cannot generate a mystical experience. Most people who tell of such experiences will tell you that they just happened, that there was no warning, no magic words or rituals to pull aside the veil. For many people such experiences are literally a once in a lifetime moment.

But, there is also a yes to the question. Yes, there is something we can do, because at least a part of the veil is of our own making. Part of what makes it hard for us to see God all around us, as Merton says, is the veil that we create.

Let me name a few of our veils. *There is the veil of busyness.* If we do not take time to smell the flowers, we certainly do not take time to look for the colors of Spirit's presence. Most of the time our minds are veiled by the preoccupations of getting and spending, coming and going, worrying and wishing. The world (the material world that is) is indeed too much with us.

There is the veil of limited assumptions. We are all shaped by the modern worldview which tells us that the only thing that is "really real" is the material world, that which can be seen, touched, heard or measured. We say that we believe in a world of spirit, at least on Sunday, but I think that most of the time we do not expect to encounter it.

There is the veil of cynicism or despair. We do not look for God's presence because we have, somewhere inside ourselves, privately given up. We may still talk the talk, but we may no longer remember the music.

So, can you pull back the veil? Yes, you can pull back some of your own veils so that Spirit does not have so much resistance to penetrate. You can open your eyes. You can open your minds. You can open your hearts.

EVERYTHING YOU WANTED IN A FATHER...AND MORE

If you then, who are evil, know how to give good gifts to your children, how much more will your Father in heaven give good things to those who ask him.

Matthew 7:11

The opening words of the Lord's Prayer probably have had more influence in setting the image of God in our minds than any words spoken before or since. We know of course that Jesus spoke as a man of his time, living in a three level universe and a patriarchal culture. Still, the fact remains that for two thousand years Christians have, as a part of both private and public worship, spoken these words: "Our Father who art in heaven."

We know that the words are symbols. We know, as Augustine reminds us, that "God is not what you imagine or what you think you understand; if you understand, you have failed." We know that, and yet our mental image of God is shaped in part by the words we use, by the metaphor, if you will, that Jesus offered as a way of helping us get a sense of the nature of the divine reality, a reality that always goes beyond words. So we can only start with the words that Jesus gave us, realizing that the word "Father" leaves out what we know of the mothering side of God, and reminding ourselves that the phrase "in heaven" only describes the transcendent side of the Spirit that is also beneath us and within us. For now, think with me about God as Father. Another day we will think about God as Mother. I promise.

To begin, then, we need to remind ourselves that Jesus himself knows that his language about God as Father is inadequate. He knows that the word calls to mind our own experience, our ups and our downs as human fathers and mothers. So he warns us that we have to expand our thinking far beyond anything that the word usually implies. "If you, who are evil, know how to give good gifts to your children, how much more will God be generous to all of his children." Think of it as the "How Much More" principle. When you pray "Our Father," when you think about God as Father, think of everything you ever wanted in a Father – and more. Let me suggest some of the ways that Jesus shows us a Father who is more, much more, than we can imagine when we think about our own parents or about ourselves as parents.

First, *Jesus shows us a Father who has enough love to go around.* The very word "our" reminds us that the one to whom we pray is Father to everyone. You cannot say "our Father" without being reminded of the people around you. You cannot say "our Father" without knowing that your relationship to God is personal but not exclusive.

Now this takes us beyond our usual thoughts about Fathers. When we were growing up we all wanted to have a kind of special relationship with our parents. We wanted to believe that we were the favorite. We competed, nicely or not so nicely, for "most favored child" status. Maybe you remember that. Maybe you have noticed it with your own children. Children have a possessive, even proprietary attitude toward their parents, a need to claim them as "mine." I heard not long ago about a mother who decided to go on a diet after she heard one of her kids bragging to a friend, "My mother is bigger than your mother."

Our possessiveness, our need to be special, our competition for parental attention – all of these are born, I believe, from our fear that there's not going to be enough

Walking to Wisdom

love to go around. If mother smiles at sister, then she loves her more than me. If daddy plays ball with brother, then he loves brother the most. This is the fear that nags at us. And because our parents were human and because we as parents are human, there is always a certain degree of validity to it. Sometimes parents *don't* have enough energy or tact or skill to give all of their children what they need when they need it.

Jesus speaks to this fear when he speaks of the father who is much more, of a God whose family is as big as the whole human family and who still knows us all by name. He shows us a God who is big enough to be the God of all people and yet personal enough to care for each of us – a God who can be *our* father and also *my* father.

It is hard to get your mind around such a thing. But if we can begin to think that way, we can also begin to see other people differently. We don't have to claim God for our church or our nation as though God could not also be the God of the Muslims or the God of the Chinese. Calling God "our Father" is the foundation for seeing other people as members of "our family." Our cherished American tradition of diversity – in religion, in culture, in ethnic background – is grounded in such a belief.

Second, *God is a Father who gives even when we don't give back.* That too is hard to imagine. We can all remember times when we weren't acting very loveable and our parents seemed to back off a bit – or more than a bit. We can also remember times when our own children were being difficult or sulky and we had a hard time staying warm and affectionate. Let's face it, it is not easy to reach out lovingly to someone who is sulking, whether that child is your child or yourself, whether the sulker is ten years old, or forty, or seventy. Human fathers and mothers sometimes find it hard to keep giving when their feelings are hurt or their patience is thin or their reserve of goodwill is low. And sometimes we are afraid that God will treat us the same way. "God won't love me if I'm bad. God won't bless me if I don't come to church." Unfortunately, just as we sometimes use that kind of threat to try to control our children, religion has sometimes tried to control us by picturing God as a kind of petulant Daddy who passes out favors to the good kids and punishes the rest.

Jesus doesn't show us that kind of Father. Remember his words? *He makes the rain to fall on the just and the unjust. His sun shines on good and evil alike.* One of the best testimonials I have heard for this church is from a person who said that it was not until she came that she discovered she wasn't going to hell. I'm sorry it took so long for her to get the message straight. Christians have often taken their own experience with controlling and spiteful fathers and assumed the same thing about God. Jesus' word is clear even though it seems too good to be true: God is a Father who gives even when we don't give back.

Again, it is not easy to grasp that God is more loving and forgiving than anything we have ever experienced. But as we begin to let that knowledge sink in, we may discover a confidence and a freedom from fear that we never imagined. If God really is the kind of God who sticks with us no matter what, then maybe we can learn how to stick with each other, and even with ourselves, no matter what. Wouldn't that be a new day?

Finally, *God is a Father who gives us freedom to find our own way.* Many people who compare God to a Father think of him as someone who wants to run everything, to make everyone conform to His eternal blueprint. That seems to be especially true of fundamentalist religions. They tend to picture a very controlling God who lays down a lot of rules and spells out how we are to keep them. Because we as parents sometimes try to control our children and often want our children to fulfill our best dreams, we may think of God in the same way. So we make God into an over-protective, over-controlling Victorian Father who wants to pick out our clothes and our friends and our life's work.

But that doesn't sound to me like a particularly good Father. That sounds like less rather than more. When I have wanted my children to think and act just like me, it has usually come out of my own insecurity, my own need to be confirmed. That's when I have been at my worst as a father. When I'm at my best as a father I want my children to find their own way, even though it may be different from my way. I want them to be true originals, not carbon copies.

I think that the Father Jesus shows us – the "How Much More" Father – is one who is not insecure or over-controlling, who gives us real freedom, entrusting us with a life to live and the gifts to live it well. The immense variety of human gifts and styles and personalities and tastes tells me that God is not interested in duplicates. Why in the world would we think that the God who created elephants and butterflies and cactus and buzzards could possibly want all human beings to think and act alike?

The implications of this are, once more, hard to grasp. This means that God loves us enough to allow us to make a terrible mess of our lives if we so choose. I can drive too fast, drink too much, pollute the air I breathe, abuse or neglect my neighbor, participate – either actively or passively – in adding to the sum total of hatred and violence that erodes our life as human beings. I am free, you are free, to misuse the gift of freedom.

But the opposite is also true. You and I are really free to make the very most of the life we are given. We are not created to be carbon copies but true originals. One of the glories of the American Dream is the fact that a group of ordinary human beings risked their lives to create a genuinely new thing, a society that had never existed beyond the dreaming stage. You and I have the opportunity to take the gift of creativity that God plants in each of us and to be literally co-creators with God. What an astonishing, frightening gift! No wonder we so often retreat into legalism. No wonder we hardly dare to believe that God is that generous with each of us.

But that is the legacy of the Father Jesus shows us, the How Much More Father. This Father is one who has enough love to go around, who loves us even when we do not love back, who gives us freedom to find our own way to use the precious gift of life.

If you then, who are evil, know how to give good gifts to your children, how much more will your Father who is in heaven give good things to those who ask Him.

How much more!

IN DEFENSE OF THE PRESBYTERIAN VIRTUES

My wife Lynn is a good Presbyterian. Even if she had not been raised one and married one, she would, because of certain deeply held values, be a solid Presbyterian. Not necessarily in her theology. Calvin might well turn over in his grave at some of her ideas, and she would probably shudder if she knew the label I am giving her (I haven't asked her yet). But her values, I insist, are Presbyterian values. Her virtues are what I believe can fairly be called Presbyterian Virtues.

I am thinking of a favorite Presbyterian phrase. It is invoked solemnly by my brothers and sisters within the church family in moments of stress. It is spoken with wry condescension by cousins to the liberal left and the rowdy right of us. The phrase, as you might guess, is *"decently and in order,"* a Presbyterian modifier if ever I heard one.

Now as our critics well know, these particular virtues can be invoked to hide a multitude of sins and pathologies. We may invoke "decency" to cover what might better be called timidity. We might whitewash as "orderly" what others might accurately perceive as "obsessive." What we like to rationalize as "decently and in order" may be seen by our critics (and even by the self-critical voice within us) as excessive concern about image, caution in the face of controversy, defense of the status quo.

But when they are virtues they are still virtues. There is something important about decency, no matter that it may sometimes be used to disguise prudery. There is something of value in a devotion to order, even though it may be turned to defensive purposes. If you ask Lynn why she insists on being on time for meetings or other appointments, she will say "because it is not thoughtful to keep people waiting." If you ask why she labors to have everything ready in advance of the arrival of guests, she will say, "so that they can enjoy the surroundings and I can enjoy the conversation without being in the kitchen."

Perhaps the most revered use of the word "decent" comes in our Declaration of Independence, when Thomas Jefferson reminds us that "a decent respect for the opinions of mankind" requires that those who are about to make a radical claim to independence state their reasons. Decency has to do with a respect for the feelings and opinions of others. We knock on a door and ask "are you decent?" We are inquiring whether our knock is an intrusion on another's privacy and whether the other's state of dress may be an offense to our senses or their modesty. We are, in other words, respecting the opinions and feelings of others. Decency does not preclude bold action. Jefferson's "decent respect for the opinions of mankind" did not keep him from signing his Declaration. It only required that he account for himself in a thoughtful and civil way.

Concern for order, at its best, is a concern for harmony. "Bringing order out of chaos" is what might be called a typically Presbyterian form of creativity. Finding a harmonious solution to the complexities of human interaction is important in our life as a community, just as finding a harmonious combination of notes and rhythms is important for a composer. One of the endearing gifts in the music of Mozart is his ability to find 'just the right note" to resolve a musical phrase. Sometimes we fail to think of order as a dimension of creativity. If so we have only to remind ourselves that such an ordering of chaos is in fact the divine work of Genesis One. When Lynn is teased for straightening pictures or correcting punctuation, she would say, I think, that she is simply sweeping back the infringing edges of chaos.

Orderliness may, of course, seem stuffy or picky. And trying to impose order on others may not be well received by those whose disorderly ways are being challenged. (The sloppy side of me wants to rebel against Lynn's attempt to manage my chaos, even while I know that I will appreciate the serenity and beauty that she creates in our home and in our life together.) Being orderly can sometimes seem stuffy or over-controlling, but it does not have to be that way. Mozart's gift for harmony did not prevent him from finding wonderful new combinations of sound or from being startlingly unconventional.

So, how do these cherished Presbyterian Virtues play their part in our daily effort to live out the purposes of God in our lives and in our common life? Well, it seems to me that we are taught by our Lord to cultivate an awareness of the feelings and thoughts of those whose lives we touch. And that means that whatever decisions we take as individuals or as a church, we take them with a decent respect for and sensitivity to those with whom we may differ. We are also called, I believe, to be the instruments by which the divine Spirit works to bring order out of chaos, to create new harmonies in our homes, our church and our community. These are Presbyterian Virtues worth keeping.

THE MOTHER OF US ALL

Then God said, "Let us make humankind in our image, according to our likeness . . . So God created humankind in his image . . . male and female he created them.
Gen. 1:26-27

Perhaps you've heard of the astronaut who returned from a voyage to outer space to be greeted by reporters. 'I've seen God," said the astronaut. Every one waited breathlessly for the revelation, and the astronaut said, "She's black."

The story reflects something of our uneasy suspicion that God may not fit our favorite images. It also reflects our awareness that men and women have somehow known that the source and Center of being that we call God must in some way be both the father and the mother of us all. The Chinese speak of "Yin" and "Yang," the masculine and feminine principle within every person. Plato used the myth of androgyne – the word means "man-woman" – to suggest that every human being is somehow incomplete until masculinity is completed by femininity and vice-versa.

Now our Judeo-Christian culture, growing as it does out of a strong patriarchal society, has almost totally excluded any acknowledgement of Mother-God. Even so, we have found a lot of ways to acknowledge that reality. The Roman Catholic tradition developed a great emphasis on Mary, so that expressions like "Mother of God" and "Queen of Heaven" certainly come very close to giving Mary a kind of divine status. And even John Calvin, with his intensely rational masculine theology, wrote, "Whoever has God for a father has the Church for a mother." For

Calvin the Church is expressing the mothering side of God. We also find popular expressions that recognize the feminine in God. We talk about "mother earth" and "dame fortune." We ascribe a kind of omniscience to her when we say, "Don't try to fool Mother Nature."

The movement to reclaim women's rights has called our attention to the heavily-weighted masculine imagery in our worship, our hymns, our prayers, our assumptions of masculine dominance in our church orders. I think there's a very important benefit for all of us, quite beyond the benefit that men and women alike have gained by a more balanced participation by women in the ministry of the church. I think we are rediscovering something about the reality of God that's been obscured by our one-sided picture. And I think that a deeper understanding of God can affect the way we see ourselves and the way we live our lives together. Look for a moment at the scripture lessons today to see what they can show us about this other side of God.

In the story of Creation in the Book of Genesis the writer says, *God created man in His own image* (or as another translation puts it, *someone like ourselves*) ...*God created man in His own image, in the image of God He created him; male and female He created them.* Now if the parallel style of Hebrew writing suggests anything, it suggests to me that "male and female" are parallel to "Image of God." It suggests that there is both a male and female dimension within the Creator and that this dual nature is reflected in human beings.

Now think about what that could mean for our notion of God as Creator. To me it suggests a continually caring, nurturing kind of God as well as one who speaks a command and breathes a life-giving breath. Do you want to see a masculine image of God as creator? Look at Michelangelo's famous painting. You can almost feel the

Walking to Wisdom

flow of energy, you can see the power. You can also get a sense of the awesome distance between the father-creator and the human creature. That picture is a valuable, powerful part of our image of God as Creator.

Now, do you want to hear an expression of the feminine element in the Creator? Listen to these lines from James Weldon Johnson's sermon/poem on the Creation:

Then God walked around, and God looked around on all that he had made. He looked at his sun, and he looked at his moon, and he looked at his little stars; He looked on his world with all its living things, And God said: I'm lonely still. Then God sat down — On the side of a hill where he could think; by a deep, wide river he sat down; With his head in his hands, God thought and thought, till he thought: "I'll make me a man!"

Up from the bed of the river God scooped the clay; and by the bank of the river He kneeled him down; And there the great God Almighty Who lit the sun and fixed it in the sky, who flung the stars to the most far corner of the night, who rounded the earth in the middle of his hand; This Great God, like a mammy bending over her baby, kneeled down in the dust toiling over a lump of clay till he shaped it in his own image;

Then into it he blew the breath of life, and man became a living soul. Amen. Amen.

Can you feel something different in that image? Can you sense the nurturing warmth? Can you feel the sustaining presence? If your God is like the clock-maker who sets things spinning and then lets them go, maybe you need to meet the mothering God of the black poet.

Now remember the lesson in which we hear something of the same balance in the words of Jesus. First we hear scathing words for the Pharisees. He calls them "snakes, whitewashed tombs, blind guides." Hard, sharp, critical words. Then, in the very next line, "Jerusalem, Jerusalem, how often would I have gathered you to myself like a mother hen!" Like a mother hen would gather her young under her wing, so Jesus says he would care for those who have turned away. This is the one whom we call the Christ, in whom we say the image of God is most fully revealed. This Jesus shows in a single incident a fully developed image of judgment and mercy, anger and tenderness, confrontation and compassion. Remember Jonah, scolding the city and sulking when it wasn't destroyed? Doesn't this Christ, in whom both male and female are fully developed, doesn't this Christ show us a better God?

Well, what can it mean? What can it mean for us to realize the feminine and the masculine within God and within ourselves? What does it mean to believe, if you will, in the "motherhood" of God? I think that for women it means a divine affirmation of their full personhood. If God is the divine father-mother who gives birth to us all, then women participate fully in the divine being – no less and no more than men.

For men it means that we can accept the feminine within ourselves and acknowledge it and enjoy it as a gift of God. Women have benefited from the women's movement by reaffirming their God-given right to be assertive. Men can benefit from the women's movement by recovering their God-given right to be tender. And they can find in the motherhood of God a divine ground for that tenderness. This means to me that men don't have to be "macho" to be real men. As a matter of fact, it means that if they are *only* macho, they are not yet real men. They haven't yet discovered a whole part of themselves as persons made in the image of God.

Finally, it can mean something for our society. An awareness of the father-mother nature of God can help us to temper our lives together. We have too long justified our aggression, our acquisitiveness, our competition with images of warlike gods. We've too long claimed God as an ally in our imperial and nationalist and religious crusades. If we are going to survive as a truly human society, we are going to have to do better than that. We are going to have to learn to temper our ambition with compassion, our conquest of outer space with a concern for inner space, our striving for success with a new sensitivity to those who share this small planet with us. Maybe the Mother God can help us behave more like a family.

A WELL KEPT SECRET

One of the better kept secrets of western Christianity is the persistence, from the earliest days of the Christian movement, of a minority within that movement who hold to some form of belief in rebirth, transmigration of souls, or, using the most common term, reincarnation. Just why this idea has remained a secret is a topic worth considering to which this essay will give only brief attention. But the fact that it has remained a secret is, to my thinking, a troubling fact. In my opinion the idea of rebirth, understood in a Christian context, can and does address some of the most difficult dilemmas of thinking persons who wish to remain true to their faith. Therefore, it seems to me that those who have come to such a view owe it to fellow Christians to share the secret.

The purpose of this essay, then, is to lay out some of the reasons that I, as a lifelong professing Christian who has worked within a mainstream Protestant denomination for 40 years of ordained ministry, have come to embrace a belief in reincarnation which seems to me to be both legitimate and valuable in my faith journey. I will try to spell out some of the reasons that I see it as *legitimate* within the Christian tradition. Then I will speak to what seems even more important; that is, why it is *valuable*.

Before addressing these two issues, let me say a word about why, in my opinion, belief in reincarnation has been, and still is, a secret among Christians. Most historians of religion would agree that the world of the Middle East in biblical times was a crossroads of many strains of religious thought. While it is beyond my expertise to speak of these strains, it is safe to say that the idea of transmigration of souls was a part of the common religious language of the day, being present in the Greek and Asian thought that colored the worldviews of the regions' peoples. The idea is present in the Bible as well, although orthodox preachers tend to ignore such instances as much as possible. For example, when the disciples ask Jesus whether he is Elijah or John the Baptist, they are assuming some kind of reincarnation. It is worth noting that Jesus does not correct their question as though it were absurd, but simply answers them by saying that "a greater than John the Baptist" has come. Again, the idea of pre-existence is common in early Christian writings, especially the Gospel of John. Concepts such as "rebirth", "resurrection" and "second coming", all essential to Christian thinking from the beginning, can be understood in a reincarnationist framework although that is not the way they are used in scripture. In the early years of the Christian movement, well respected teachers wrote about pre-existence and transmigration. Origen, one of the most brilliant of the early church's theologians, assumed pre-existence in his extensive commentaries and other writings.

So, if the idea of rebirth was a part of the common parlance, if some form of reincarnation can be thought of as simply a different venue, so to speak, for the Christian idea of an afterlife, why did the idea disappear from the church's radar screen? Historians have looked at the theological battles of the early centuries and suggested many possible answers, most of which are beyond the scope of this essay. In brief, however, it can be said that there was among some of the most influential of the early fathers a great concern for unity among the scattered Christian communities. Such unity could, it was felt, be best served by developing an approved body of writings out of which all Christians would be taught – a sourcebook or canon. Irenaeus, who held such a view, proposed his own such list, which he modestly called the "canon of truth". Those who accepted this canon for instruction would come to be counted among the true believers. Those who chose to learn from other writings came to be called "choosers" or "heretics", from the Greek word *haeresis*, meaning "a choice". What first was used as a term for defining those who made a choice became, as we know, a term by which those persons were labeled as outsiders and finally stigmatized as threats to be expelled from the Christian community. And when in the time of Constantine the church as an institution became identified with the state, such choosing became a risky thing indeed.

Of course we no longer burn heretics at the stake. But the weight of two thousand years of church tradition does, I believe, tempt Christians who choose to read other books and think other thoughts to keep them to themselves, or at least to share them only with like minded "choosers" who will explore such thoughts with them rather than calling them names. So much for the "why" of the well kept secret. Let me move on to two more basic questions. That is, *how* is reincarnation a legitimate and valuable part of my belief?

I believe that reincarnation may be a legitimate concept within orthodox Christian belief for two reasons. *First, reincarnation is not inconsistent with Christian concepts related to the afterlife.* I do not suggest that everyone need agree to this. Certainly the dominant biblical picture of the afterlife suggests otherwise. However, this biblical picture is not at all clear or consistent, nor does it seem to me to represent a fundamental part of Christian belief. For Christians belief in the central place of Jesus in demonstrating victory over death is a given. However, the nature and extent of that new life is far less clearly defined. In the synoptic gospels, Jesus speaks in stories, using the imagery of the apocalyptic of his day. In the Fourth Gospel his words about "eternal" life suggest a *quality* of life that begins in the present. Similarly, in the Gospel of Thomas, he speaks often of a Kingdom that is growing within us in the here and now rather than in another time and place. While Paul's writings attempt to go a bit further in describing the afterlife (e.g. I Cor.15) he does not seem interested in spelling out a total framework. His letters, in general, address themselves to specific concerns of specific Christian communities; they are not philosophical treatises. In addition, Paul's assumptions about an imminent return of the Christ make him relatively indifferent to the business of extended growth into the future. From earliest times Christian belief about the afterlife has interwoven the Jewish idea of resurrection with the Greek concept of immortality. Over the centuries Christian theology has struggled with both ideas; neither has claimed clear ownership for all Christians. Reincarnation, as I understand it, is not incompatible with either.

Second, reincarnation is a legitimate alternative for Christians because it *preserves and even enhances principles primary to Jesus' teaching.* Jesus calls upon people to open themselves to the rule of God in their lives, to live more and more as citizens of the Kingdom. His stories and images constantly reinforce the idea of that rule as a growing spiritual presence that is expressed through loving relationships with God and neighbor. He is interested, in brief, in the journey of the soul toward spiritual wholeness. The where and the when and the "how long" of that journey is never spelled out, nor is it primary in Jesus' teaching. But Jesus makes clear that his Way is one that fulfills the divine law or purpose, not one that denies it.

As I understand it, reincarnation involves a process of evolutionary growth over a number of rebirths, wherein the soul returns to continue its journey, benefiting from previous growth as well as experiencing the consequences of previous failures. This notion of consequence, traditionally called *karma*, simply spells out the biblical notion that "we reap what we sow". Geddes MacGregor has written persuasively of what he calls the "christening of karma", pointing out that Judaeo-Christian tradition never speaks of abolishing the divine law but insists that spiritual maturity comes through growth, not some sudden abrogation of all consequences by divine fiat. The preservation of the divine moral law is a cornerstone of the concept of karma and of reincarnation.

But does this karma negate the Christian understanding of grace? In my opinion, not at all. The grace of God that I see revealed in Christ simply removes the obstacle that has kept me from growing toward spiritual maturity. Grace is not an abrogation of the divine law but the means by which I may grow toward more fully living out that law. And I may have to rediscover that grace again and again, both in this life and in future lives. Traditional Christian theology has struggled to resolve the puzzle created by the conflict between divine grace, which has the power to preserve us, and divine law, which none of us has come close to living out in one lifetime. The doctrine of purgatory was one attempt, providing a place for purging (not punishment) wherein the person who died in a state of incompleteness might continue in his spiritual growth. Dante's classic image of the seven story ascent through the levels of *purgatorio* depicts the pilgrimage of the soul, growing toward liberation from the seven deadly sins. What the doctrine of purgatory assigns to an intermediate state, reincarnation places in the arena where previous growth or failure to grow has taken place; that is, physical, earthly life.

Reincarnation, then, as I understand it, is simply an alternative way to conceive of the soul's journey. It is consistent with Jesus' teaching and with the church's view of an afterlife. For reasons that are unclear, it has always been a concept that makes people in western civilizations very uncomfortable. Perhaps it has to do with the western concern for individual identity and a fear that such identity will be lost with repeated incarnations. Perhaps the uneasiness in ecclesiastical circles has to do with the fact that the soul's journey is seen in very personal and individual ways, with no absolute need for a mediating agent such as church or sacrament (MacGregor and Elaine Pagels both suggest that churchly concerns with Gnostic thinking in early Christianity had to do with issues of ecclesiastic political power). At any rate, I see no reason to dismiss the concept simply because it makes some people uncomfortable. The whole idea of afterlife- heaven, hell, purgatory and all - makes a lot of people uncomfortable. To me, reincarnation is not only a legitimate understanding for Christians, but it is valuable in dealing with some of the most difficult problems for faith.

Reincarnation helps me make sense of two important issues: *the issue of justice and the issue of "premature" death.* I have already touched on the issue of justice. Many persons who want to believe in some kind of divine justice have a hard time with both of the traditional solutions of Christian theology to the question of what happens to "incomplete" souls at the time of their death. As I have mentioned, Catholic theology has solved the problem with the doctrine of purgatory. If a person has a long way to go toward spiritual maturity but manages to be baptized before death, he/she may spend some time being brought up to speed, so to speak, in an intermediate state called purgatory. Just how that purging happens seems to depend in part on the prayers of the faithful here on earth, which in turn are related to certain churchly activities. Protestant theology, in reaction to what seemed an artificial, ecclesiastically controlled process for dispensing God's grace, rejected purgatory in favor of an opposite position. In most Protestant thought, the immature believer is suddenly and immediately cleansed of all sin at the time of death. Thus God's grace is preserved but a new problem is introduced, the presence of many "incomplete" believers in a totally egalitarian heaven. Protestantism, in avoiding the intermediate step of purgatory, leaves no place for souls to grow.

This picture, while obviously something of a caricature of both positions, still captures, I believe, something of the dilemma that many thinking persons encounter when they consider traditional Christian teaching. The dilemma may be stated this way: How can I take seriously the fact that spiritual growth is something that obviously requires more than a single lifetime, even a long one? How can I, at the same time believe that the consequences of violations of divine law are simply wiped out for those who are fortunate enough to hear and respond to the message of God's grace in Christ? How can the eternal destiny of a soul created and beloved of God be subject to the limitations and accidents of a single lifetime without doing serious damage to the divine purpose? Does it make sense to think that a wise and loving God would create precious souls only to waste so much of their potential in such a chancy thing as a single lifetime? It doesn't make much sense to me.

Reincarnation introduces the doctrine of the second chance. Or third. Or fourth. Not only do I need more time for growth, God wants me to have more time. Not only must I work through the consequences of past failures, I have the opportunity to build on past successes, to become a genuinely better, more loving, more spiritually mature person. I can and must grow toward this maturity in the very arena in which past mistakes and successes happened. Not in order to earn my salvation. That is already a given, for God in God's grace has claimed me for eternity. Just knowing that eternal claim can free me from much preoccupation with legalistic efforts at self-validation as well as from the despair of feeling eternally ignored or rejected. I do not "work out my salvation" in order to earn something, but in order to become more whole (*salus*) which is, after all, the purpose for which I was created. I like to think of life as a school for the soul. And I think that we will go to that school for as many lifetimes as it may take to graduate. I think that God is eternally patient with us, so that we may flunk out and repeat, or go through the motions of rote learning, or settle down and learn our lessons. The pace of the process is, literally, as *we* will.

Reincarnation also addresses the issue of "premature" death. How are we to understand the fate of the stillborn child, the young victim of illness, the thirty year old killed by war or accident in the prime of life? Even if we assume that those persons are embraced by God and held in some safe heaven, how do we deal with their tragically brief time on the stage, their possibilities for growth cut short? The fact of untimely or early death is a double tragedy, a loss for loved ones and a loss for the person whose only opportunity is suddenly (and unfairly) brought to a halt.

For me, the concept of reincarnation helps make some sense of such losses. While the idea of a second chance does little to comfort the bereaved family, it does hold out the hope that the child or young adult will not be totally deprived of the chance that those of us have who are granted our three score and ten (although this seems short enough for those of us who find ourselves approaching or passing the magic number). With reincarnation there is no premature death for the soul, only a change in venue, so to speak. There are no souls of babies floating in limbo, but reborn souls who get a chance to start again with the same opportunity for growth as others. Were I to lose a child I would cherish that hope. Because I have lost young friends, I am in fact glad to believe that they have found new arenas in which to test themselves and enjoy themselves in this beautiful and difficult world.

For the reasons I have given, the concept of reincarnation has become a valuable part of my belief as a Christian. I cannot prove it any more than my fellow, more orthodox believers can prove heaven or hell (or, for that matter, any more than my materialist friends can disprove it). I have not spoken of the evidence which has led me to believe that reincarnation is likely. In brief, I can say that I am impressed by what I have read and heard about past life recollection (Ian Stevenson, Brian Weiss, many others) near death experiences (Raymond Moody, Melvin Morse) and memory (Morse). I have discovered that I am, as a believer in reincarnation, in the company of a number of thoughtful persons over the centuries, and that the collective weight of their experience and wisdom is not easily dismissed. For the purposes of this essay I have tried simply to share the discovery and the sense of resolution, satisfaction and, yes, comfort that it has brought me.

EVERYONE WANTS THE LAST WORD

I still have many things to say to you, but you cannot bear them now. When the spirit of truth comes, he will guide you into all the truth.

John 16: 12-13

Everyone wants the last word. The last word in fashion, the last word in an argument, the last word on the weather, even the last word in theology. There is something about us that is eager to possess the ultimate. So we spend money we don't have to buy the outfit or gadget we don't need. Somehow we feel better if we own the last word.

We want to have the last line in every debate. So he makes his speech with his hand on the doorknob. And then she follows him out on the porch and offers her parting shot, punctuating her ultimatum, if possible, with a slamming door. We stay up later than we should, checking the final update on the weather in North Carolina or the political weather in Washington or the military weather in Iraq. Somehow we go to sleep a little easier if we've heard the last word.

There is even a theological discipline – of course – that means, literally, "last word". The discipline is called *eschatology*, the study of last things. And people eagerly write books (and other people eagerly buy them) offering a guaranteed glimpse of how it is all going to turn out. Why are we so eager to possess the last word? How likely, really, are we to get it? And what would it take to learn to live without it?

I

Why do we feel that we need the last word? I think it has to do with wanting a measure of control. If I have the last word in an argument, the ball is in her court. If I have heard the final weather report, then maybe nothing surprising will happen while I'm not watching. If I own the last word in cars or electronics or clothing, no one will get ahead of me. And of course, if I have the last word from God, then my soul is secure.

It seems very hard for us to stay open to the possibility that God's dream for the world is still unfolding. Every religious group wants to believe that God has finally spoken the Last Word. And amazingly, it just happens to be the word that God spoke to *them*. There is a name for that too. It is called "supercessionism". That is, my religion supercedes all religions that came before it.

You know how it goes. The Jews are convinced that God chose them as His people and gave them a land forever, which of course supercedes any claim made by previous residents or future ones. Some Christians like to believe that God's revelation in Christ not only fulfills the faith of Abraham but makes it no longer valid. Many Muslims call their man Mohammed the "seal of the prophets", meaning that he has the last prophetic word superceding all others.

And so on. Some orthodox Protestants still think that God had his last say somewhere in the 16th century. Some scientific materialists are as certain as any fundamentalist that their worldview wipes out all earlier world views. Believers in a literal, apocalyptic view of the Book of Revelation are sure that they have an accurate map of the end of the world. All of us long for the security of the Last Word.

II

How likely are we to know the last word? Not very. Listen to the words of Jesus: "there is a lot more for you to learn but you cannot bear it now. When the Spirit of truth comes He will guide you." Later the writer of the gospel puts it this way: "there are many other things that Jesus did; if every one of them were written down, I suppose that the world itself could not contain the books that would be written."

Jesus was always leaving the door open, always warning people not to claim that they had a corner on God's concerns or God's purposes. "I have other sheep", he said, "who are not of this fold." As to the end of the world, he said more than once that "no one, not even the Son, knows the hour."

When you take a look at who we are and what we are expecting, the idea of having the last word is a little presumptuous. The psalmist, who had a good perspective on the matter, put it this way: "When I look at your heavens, the work of your fingers, the moon and the stars that you have established; what are human beings that you are mindful of them, mortals that you care for them?" The psalmist is amazed that God has made human beings "just a little lower than the angels," amazed that God pays special attention to these tiny inhabitants of a tiny planet. So why, he might ask, should we expect that we should have the last word on anything? The psalmist would agree, I think, with a later student of nature named Thoreau, who put it this way: "The universe is wider than our views of it."

Indeed it is. The universe and its Creator are wider and greater than we can get our minds around. Our attempts to speak God's last word on the world or even on our little corner of it say a lot more about our insecurity and our arrogance than about God's creation or God's dream. The discoveries of modern science should make us cautious about assuming that our knowledge of God's universe and its human travelers ended in biblical days. And the wisdom of the ancient world about the world of Spirit should make modern scientists cautious about assuming that their present worldview is a final and accurate picture of that universe.

The last word does not belong to Malachi or to the Revelation of John or to Mohammed or to John Calvin or to Albert Einstein or to Tim Lahaye. Or to me. The last word belongs to God. I believe that that should be enough.

III

What would it take for us to live without the last word? Well, I believe that we can learn to live without the last word when we are willing to trust that God is good and that God's last word to us is a word of grace. It is not necessary to know the last chapter of a book when you trust the skill and wisdom of the author. Let me change the metaphor. It is possible to look forward to the end of a piece of music if you trust the creativity of the composer and his ability to make beauty.

Some of you know that I love the music of Mozart. I have no musical training to speak of, but I can tell you why I love it. First, I love the way he can take the sound of every instrument and every voice and weave them all together in constantly changing and always elegant patterns. Second, I love the way the music always seems to be going somewhere, one theme evolving gracefully into another. Finally, I am able to trust that even those moments in Mozart's music that seem unresolved will have their resolution and that even the silences will add meaning and beauty to the whole.

It seems to me that this can be a way for us to think

about how we may entrust ourselves to God. Think of yourself as part of a vast ensemble of players who are trying to let their music be guided by the Spirit of one who is creating a masterwork out of the melodies – and lack of melody – that they make. There will be discordant notes. There will be clashing dissonance, especially when one instrument tries to overpower another. There will even be silences – call them rests – when it may seem that the whole huge ensemble has lost the thread. But even in those silences, our trust is that God the creative Spirit is never going to give up on the musicians God has created or on the music God has dreamed for us.

What we have played thus far might sound like an unfinished symphony. But I believe that the last note, like the first, belongs to God. And I believe that the last note, like the first, will be good.

SO, HOW LONG IS THE WALK?

Sure, he that made us with such large discourse, looking before and after, gave us not that capability and godlike reason to fust in us unused.   Hamlet

In my father's recollections the walk to wisdom seemed to go on and on. As I have reflected on what seems to me the likely ways of a loving and creative divine Spirit, I find myself agreeing with Hamlet. Why, I have asked myself, would such a loving God give us one brief hour upon this elaborate stage within which most of our potential could only "fust unused"?

While I am not sure just what it means to fust, I suspect that Shakespeare does not think of it in a kindly way. Neither do I. Neither, I believe, does God. So I have come to the conviction that God, for our walk to wisdom, has given us as long as it takes. With Teilhard de Chardin I believe that we are spiritual beings having a human experience. If that human experience is in fact the school in which we are placed to grow in the ways that physical challenges and personal relationships seem uniquely fitted to test and encourage, then it seems divinely right that school be in session for as long as we need to learn our lessons. I suppose that some heavenly spiritual plane might also be a place for growth. But for humans, what better place than this beautiful but bumpy earthly road? I think that we will meet each other many more times in our long walk to wisdom.

Printed in the United States
42863LVS00003B/1-24